Dedicated to those who saved lives at sea, risking their own.
To all souls at the RNLI in the United Kingdom and
the KNRM in the Netherlands and their 200th anniversary.

WIND, TIDE & OAR

WIND

Encounters with

TIDE &

engineless sailing

OAR

HUW WAHL, WIEBE RADSTAKE, STEVIE HUNT,
RICHARD TITCHENER, MIKE JACKSON,
JESSICA TAGGART ROSE, EMMA RAULT, JUDE BRICKHILL,
ARTUR C. JASCHKE, GREG POWLESLAND,
ROSE MAY RAVETZ *&* CATHARINA VERGEER

the new
**Menard
press**

Contents

"The fishermen know that the sea is dangerous and the storm terrible, but
they have never found these dangers sufficient reason for remaining ashore."
— VINCENT VAN GOGH

"Hark, now hear the sailors cry,
Smell the sea, and feel the sky,
Let your soul & spirit fly, into the mystic."
— VAN MORRISON

"Go small, go simple, go now"
— LARRY PARDEY, *Cruising in Seraffyn*

"The sea is a great master but a poor slave"
— Witness of the tragedy of the *Solomon Browne*
lifeboat at Mousehole, Cornwall

"Poolster

Hij is boven de zee

zei mijn vader –

de poolster is hij

op hem varen wij."

— HUUB OOSTERHUIS

"The wind bloweth where it listeth, and thou hearest the sound thereof,

but canst not tell whence it cometh, and whither it goeth."

— ST JOHN, 3:8

"The tide flows in, the tide flows out;

twice every day returning"

— TRADITIONAL BALLAD

Preface by the publisher

Writing, filming and sailing have much in common. Even publishing—at least the way I go about it—may fit into this collection of activities. The preliminary tool is, namely, intuition and a certain intrepidity to improvise. Aside from a few skills and the motivation—or obsession—you have for the task, intuition is the flow, the current, the tide, if you like, omnipresent throughout the process and eternally returning. But should one trust their intuition? Well, you should certainly not ignore it. Especially if you are without an engine.

When Huw Wahl, the director of the film *Wind, Tide & Oar*, approached me, I'd never met him before. He found out I was a publisher and author, living on a historic sailing barge, through a mutual friend of ours, who put us in touch with one another. And when at last we met, and Huw told me he was working on an analogue film about engineless sailing, I understood why Gareth, our friend, had seen a link. When Huw revealed that he did not want the film to be a documentary, nor an art film, activist manifesto, or feature film, I understood him even better. I intuitively tuned into his vision, and since my business is books, it only seemed logical there would be a book with the film.

Pretty much from the first conversation we had, we talked about this sense of intuition, and when and how to use it while you are working on a creation with people, which is subsequently shared with an audience. Lots of conversations were to follow, most of these recorded and collected, shared and sent across the English Channel via voice notes. For I live, work and write between countries; I live on the water between the UK and mainland Europe.

Both sides of the shore are strongly connected by maritime history. It is no coincidence that the rescue societies of both the UK and the Netherlands (the Royal National Lifeboat Institution and the Royal Dutch Rescue Society) celebrate their 200th anniversary this year. This book is therefore dedicated to both institutions, which have been saving lives at sea for two centuries with a group of seemingly fearless and gallant volunteers. Two hundred years ago there were no engines! They would set out against the wind and tide, with oars and in sloops made of wood. Risking—and sometimes losing—their own lives.

If the film were to display the visual narrative of how and why people today go sailing without an engine, then I would work on a book containing the written story—the two complement each other. Thus, here within are accounts of some of the sailors featured in the film, and others who have experience sailing, poets and practitioners, authors and amateurs.

This book, in a similar way to Huw's idea about his film, was not intended to become just one thing. It is about stories, experiences and encounters. With winds, tides and sometimes oars. With gulls and garbage, with currents and gales, with songs and swells, with dreams and disasters.

I do indeed live on a barge; however, we don't sail very often on our home. More frequently we sail on our 1933 wooden sloop rigged yacht, built by the surgeon and sailor, Harrison Butler, for 'easy cruising on the Solent', the water between England and the Isle of Wight. Well, I am sure she can handle it, but as for me, I haven't tried it yet. And I certainly wouldn't set out without an engine! Our 1927 Dutch barge also has a massive stinking diesel engine in the back of the hull, which, I must say, I am very attached to, if not reliant on. In the Netherlands, where she is moored, regulations rule over intuition, and it is simply not allowed to 'sail' without having an engine built in or an outboard motor on your vessel. Whether you use it or not is up to the skipper. We use it, always, when mooring or maneuvering the countless bridges and locks, or innumerable other vessels, especially in summer, when the waters of the Netherlands look like a sailing theme park.

Engineless sailing is the most sustainable way of travelling, whether for transportation or pleasure. With regards to sustainability, Wiebe Radstake opted for an electric engine on a traditional Dutch flat-bottomed barge. He was the first one in the Netherlands to do so. When I went sailing with him, I hardly noticed the engine was running. It seemed almost as quiet as the wind. The Dutch barges are closely related in design to the Thames sailing barges, without a keel but with leeboards to keep them from drifting sideways. Richard Titchener and his partner, Hilary Halajko, not only run the Sea-Change Sailing Trust charity but also work, dedicated and skillfully, on one of those Thames sailing barges called the *Blue Mermaid*. I simply adore Thames barges. They are a sturdy, reliable vessel, easy to handle, and remarkably agile for such a bulky design. She's cleverly designed and no engine is needed at all. Sailing along the Suffolk coast is a treat. Even in high season, it hasn't quite turned into a theme park yet.

During the Engineless Sailing Jolly, an engineless sailing event organised by sailor, writer and filmic collaborator Rose May Ravetz, we sailed from Pin Mill to Harwich and back with almost the whole crew now featured in the film, as well as in the book. It was a marvellous sight from the shore, and on the water it was even better. I was lucky to sail with the crew on board the *Blue Mermaid*.

There I met, amongst many others, Jude Brickhill and her husband, Jonno. They told me about their extraordinary adventures living and sailing with their whole family, from South Africa to England, on their 72-foot boat, *Guide Me*, built in 1911. Never with an engine.

The sailing community is a strong one and survives on shared narratives. Skills, but also stories about pride and joy, ideals and beliefs, are shared across the globe and its vast oceans. There is a saying: "a thousand skippers, a thousand stories"—not an untrue statement. There are so many variables in tides and winds alone, imagine those in experience and the subsequent stories. Some of them are heroic, some of them are humble; all adhere to a way of life, to a mission.

Sailors, in a similar way to writers, perhaps, and eccentric filmmakers, have the ability to feel strong kinship through these narratives, without ever having met in real life. I feel I have been friends with Emma Rault for some time, but we have never actually met. And when I met Rose May Ravetz for the first time, it was *as if* I had met her before.

This book is for everyone, not just for sailors, as every story can open up new dimensions with new adventures, exploring new horizons, both in reality as well as in our imagination.

You don't need an engine for that; you can simply trust your intuition.

Welcome aboard!

ELTE RAUCH,
Amsterdam–London, 2024

Where Sailing and Filmmaking Meet

Huw Wahl

"You distort the answer simply by asking the question"

— JEAN ROUCH

I am chasing *Guide Me* down the river Helford in Cornwall. She is a 1911 Looe Lugger owned by the Brickhill family, who once sailed her all the way to South Africa, via Brazil. From a vantage point near Trebah beach, I film her lug rig and wooden hull gliding past in silence, running with the tide and a little breeze. The crew moor up near Durgan, and I spend the rest of the afternoon walking the coast path out towards the river mouth, looking for spots to film from the next morning. They are due to leave at 5am, setting sail for the biannual Looe Lugger Regatta, where *Guide Me* will feel quite at home.

After a night in the van I gather my gear sleepily and open the door to the darkness. Down on the coast path again, after trudging through muddy fields with my head torch lighting the way, the sun begins to shine some milky light onto the scene, and I find a spot to sit. I am early, and *Guide Me* late to set off, so I have an hour at the top of the hill at Mawnan to take continuous light metre readings as the sun gets brighter, change filters, and clean my lenses.

As I see the heavy lug sails in the distance hoisted upwards, my body responds with its own movement. I feel driven by an awareness of possibility, an impulse to adjust to the change that is inevitable in anything I might capture. Boats, by their nature, are also continually responding, and the trajectory sailors plan is in constant adjustment; I have to be alert, and ready to choose the shots that feel right from the ones that don't. Although the process can be hectic, and there's often a tension before the action, once you are moving this melts away, and it's possible to feel present in the flow of what is happening around you.

Even knowing it is like this, an improvisation of sorts, one still tries to make plans. The previous afternoon I devised a shot list in my head and the points at which I would change the 100ft rolls of film. In my clockwork 16mm camera, each roll lasts about two and a half minutes, with each wind allowing twenty-five seconds of shooting before I need to rewind. All this needs to be diligently taken into account, yet I also know that once things begin, everything changes. The preparation is as much about flexibility as anything else.

Improvising and responding intuitively, whilst at the same time being overly prepared; this is the foundation of what the act of filming is for me, and from what I now know about sailing, it is also what enables an engineless sailor to survive.

And so *Guide Me* leaves the river mouth, and in the space between plan and response, a wonderful shot presents itself of her sailing into the sun, a trail of water behind and the horizon ahead. The shot is obvious, but I don't worry about it being clichéd—which is what I could think if I was *thinking*—because it gives me goose bumps as I line it up. I press the shutter and hear the film roll, deciding to shoot for the whole length of the wind. The feeling is one of peace.

Rose, do you remember my shock at how far *Defiance* heeled over going into the wind, me on the tiller thinking it would tip right over, with you calmly telling me it was a long way from capsizing? Or going into that marina on the river Orwell with the engine roaring, and the clutch not engaging properly? We turned around and around trying to dock, and after several attempts gave up and left unsuccessful. Or me swimming next to the boat when it was moored up, just about keeping up with the tide, a line out the side to drag myself back at the last moment before being swept away.

I had no terminology for sailing then—it all felt hilariously free.

What ... you can just "go where you want"?

What ... there are no sides of the "road"?

What ... you just anchor "there"?

What ... you can just get up and sail to another country?

It was questions like these that filled my head when we came together for a few days in 2020, my sister and I, on her boat, *Defiance*, a 23-foot gaff-rigged cutter. Rose was attempting to live on this tiny vessel through winter. It had no toilet and no fridge. Her tender (the small boat she used to get ashore) had no engine. She had to time her trips to land to get supplies with the tides, or else row for over half an hour, or more, if the tide was against her. Mud was a big part of her life, as was struggle. I, on the other hand, was dealing with the mud of being an artist, attempting to live through my work in film. Both of us stubbornly holding onto our ideals.

During those five days aboard *Defiance*, as we navigated the river Stour with no concrete plan aside from testing the boat's sailing capabilities, the sense of a film began to emerge between us. Rose wanted to remove her engine, inspired by her friend Stevie, who had taken the engine out of his own 42-foot steel yacht. She told me she was going to do the same. She had a hunch it was right, but the reasons were various and at that time hazy, mostly intuitive. A desire to avoid fossil fuels was central, just as it had been during her four years hitchhiking on boats around the world age nineteen, but there was also a desire to learn the skills that she felt were being forgotten, and be part of the traditions in danger of being lost. Yet what really stood out was a strong sense of resistance. The engineless sailor has to constantly justify why their choice isn't dangerous, egotistic or stupid. Rose wanted to defend engineless sailing against those who had little understanding of what is possible when such skills are present.

During those days on water, I began to make clumsy connections between analogue filmmaking and engineless sailing. Rose helped in trying to put a finger on what sailing felt like, while I tussled with what filmmaking meant to me; it was very hard for both of us to do, and trying to put words to the experiences somehow made them less vibrant, less vital.

But we kept trying, and this is how it all began, the idea of making a film centred on engineless sailing. It arose from a mutual exploration, becoming the space in which we could try and get closer to the experience, not to name it, but with the intention of feeling it even stronger within ourselves, tuning into it, and hoping that it would help us better understand our respective struggles.

My filmmaking and Rose's sailing met on *Defiance*. But also, perhaps, *in* Defiance.

Several months later I am onboard *Birubi*, a Bermudian rigged ketch, with Stevie, the friend of my sister, who had removed his engine and has just launched his boat after a six-year restoration. We glide silently through Ipswich lock gate at 4am in the pitch black, and the lock keeper shouts down to us:

"Are you, er, under wind power?"

"Yes," Stevie shouts back.

"For future reference, don't come through the lock under sail. The rules and regs say you can't."

"Okay, I did have a read of the bylaws and the terms and conditions and I couldn't find a reference to that," Stevie replies.

The man pauses for a moment, obviously considering his options, before simply saying, "You should have been told really."

"Okay, do you know where I'd be able to look that up, please?" Stevie asks defiantly.

"Not off the top of my head," comes a quiet reply, before changing the subject quickly to confirm the boat's name.

Minutes later we pass heavy industry next to the river on our right-hand side. The glowing lights of diggers meddle with giant mounds of loud aggregate, and a big building churns out thick smoke.

"This," Stevie says, pointing incredulously at everything on the shore, "is what that guy wants the world to *look* and *sound* like."

The following day, as Stevie skilfully rows me ashore with my bags of film equipment precariously piled up in his creaking tender, he begins to tell me about the "machinations" of his brain on land, where his mind tends to create problems and he generally feels less at ease with himself. He contrasts this with how he feels when sailing, where he is "completely and entirely occupied" with the multitude of things he has to think about, and which are necessary to stay safe.

Though initially counterintuitive to me, Stevie explains he finds more solace without an engine than with one. His reasons for sailing in this way are manifold: he doesn't like the reliance on a complex and prone-to-failure mechanism, the burden of carrying numerous spare parts, and being reliant on other people to help him fix it. He is unhappy at the sensation of pushing through rather than going with the natural flow, hindering his ability to keenly perceive the boat's needs and the changing weather, which sometimes means not going anywhere at all. He feels it as a personal failure if, when sailing on a boat with an engine, he has to turn it on. In essence, engines, for Stevie, do not bring peace, nor independence. Without one he can only do what the wind or weather or tide allows him to do. His options are aligned with his surroundings, and he is much more aware of the environmental resistances encountered.

I had to work with these resistances a lot when making the film, where the desire in me did not match the reality of what was forecast or occurring, or with the sailors' decisions in response to them. Just as many shots were lost due to sailors telling me we weren't sailing because the weather had changed, or the boat simply wasn't ready, as were lost due to the film running out, or me not having wound the camera in time.

Whenever I fed these frustrations back to Rose, who had quickly become my sailing oracle, she would say something like: "You have to know what to push, and what not to push. Go with it, rather than resisting."

Acceptance seemed a big part of the process of sailing without an engine and, by proximity, it began to become a big part of my filmmaking too. This is not to say frustrations were not present. Just as I would swear at a sudden squall as it sent me running for cover and ruined a potential shot, the sailor could bemoan the wind dropping. We both knew we could do nothing about it, nor control it, but it didn't stop a vexed reaction. On the flip side, when the forces aligned and allowed, we could both move and respond in a way that felt entirely free, and this was joyous. I could see we became truly part of the world in these moments, and deeply connected in its making.

In the mid-20th century, Jean Rouch, a French filmmaker and anthropologist, revolutionised documentary filmmaking by introducing the concept of the 'participant camera' in his work. This transformative approach embodies a way of being when using a camera, urging the filmmaker to actively respond to the changes in the scenes in front of them. It is an enmeshment of the filmmaker and the technology they use, encouraging them to become not just observers, but active participants in the world around them. To this concept we could add the 'participant sailor', who must tune into the changing environment, read the water and the sky, continually adjust the sails, and, without imposing their will onto the boat, use their mastery to persuade it in the best way they can to get to their destination. In the flow, they must both work out what needs pushing and what doesn't.

Also vital to Rouch's practice was the idea of the camera as a catalyst. He saw the gaze of the lens as having the potential of encouraging something to happen that might not usually occur, and in this way, altering the terms of the pro-filmic event—defined in cinema as anything that happens within the frame the camera is capturing. The presence of the filmmaker and their equipment, then, becomes part of the 'truth' that the camera records. On the flipside, Rouch was keenly aware of the traps that the rapid development of technology can provide, with Mike Eaton writing that "the technological possibilities for self-effacement offered to the ethnographic film maker are systematically refused by Rouch in the inscription of the personal and the subjective into the body of the film text" (Eaton, *Anthropology–Reality–Cinema: The Films of Jean Rouch*, 1979, p. 44). While Rouch engaged with new developments, such as synchronous sound in his work, and the innovative use of handheld 16mm cameras to capture spontaneous and authentic moments, he critically assessed technological advancements, particularly in relation to his broader concept of embodiment, subjectivity, and the dangers of self-effacement.

In today's context, effacing oneself from one's surroundings has become easier than ever. The digital world has provided us, like Rouch, with many new exciting possibilities, while at the same time offering many traps to fall into. While analogue filmmakers and engineless sailors are not necessarily primitives or purists (considering the possibility that an engineless sailor might use a smartphone or carry GPS navigation, and an analogue filmmaker may digitise footage or edit their work on a computer), their desire is to critically navigate new technologies, always questioning whether these technologies help them become more present or result in a disconnection from the world and a greater distance from their experience. Ultimately, what they desire is to participate wholly, rather than slipping away into a screen, passive and unresponsive.

When I press the shutter trigger on my analogue camera, I can feel the pulse of film as it runs through the gate, I can hear the spring winding down, and unless I want to waste the expensive material, I must really tune into the event occurring in front of me. Precisely because I cannot review the footage in the field, I must keep the images in my head, like memories or ghosts, and if I run out of film, well, I have to accept the shoot is over.

Using film allows me to feel these pressures in a heightened way, and the practicalities of time-limited rolls and the expense of the stock demand that I do a lot of editing 'in camera'. I have to be alert, switched on, tuned in, and always deciding what to shoot and what not to shoot. I've observed that this is also true of the engineless sailor, who, in the moment of action, is attuned to an intuitive rhythm, editing their actions in accordance with the environment around them.

During one shoot on Harwich Ha'penny Pier, a young sailor called Henry asked me: "How do you know *when* to shoot then?"

"That's the big unanswerable question," I said, "but I think ultimately it's about feeling."

Equally, how does a sailor know when to tack or to trim the sail this way or that? Once they have a good amount of technical know-how and skill engrained in the body, what's equally important is that the body is also open to feeling. Just as I had to feel when it was right to film *Guide Me* going down the Helford and out to open sea, without allowing thoughts to cloud my mind.

Of course, this does not always happen, and things do not always come together or align.

Just as the film might run out exactly as a perfect sequence of shots becomes apparent, sometimes the wind changes, and we don't make it in time for the tide, having to anchor and wait until our next opportunity. Yet it's in these moments that presence and patience are key. In the balance of forces, and with the embodied knowledge and skill of how to navigate them, we keep ourselves safe, so we do not run aground.

After being on *Defiance* that first time, I read Alan Watts' book *Tao: The Watercourse Way*. It became a guiding text that I carried with me throughout the project. There is a section where he discusses the various translations of the first line of the *Tao Te Ching*—a text written around 400BC and a foundation of Taoism, an ancient Chinese philosophy—which is usually rendered as "The Tao which can be spoken of is not the eternal Tao." He makes the point that the original ideogram for "be spoken of" contains in itself Tao and can be translated in a myriad of ways. My favourite, because it always felt most relevant to sailing, is "the force that is forced isn't the true force". An unforced force is something entirely vital, in my opinion, to both practices of sailing and filmmaking.

From an original seed of intention, an often mystic vision—the start of the journey—through to full growth—an arrival—there is the kernel of intention that needs to be nurtured and cared for rather than pushed.

This is where filmmaking and sailing meet.

Catching Stories on the Wind

Wiebe Radstake
Translated from the Dutch by *Emma Rault*

C all me a gatherer of tales, call me a skipper, call me a romantic. But don't call me an entrepreneur or a business owner—that would kill the story.

From a journal:

"I woke up off Yrseke, with the lights of the Port of Antwerp blinking in the distance and the first morning glow coming over the Tholen dyke on the far side of the estuary. As I walked around Yrseke, the town came to life. A small market, illuminated with string lights, was setting up around the little church. Loud shouts of good morning in the broad Zeeland dialect rang out in the narrow streets. On my way back, the sun rose over the water. The light falling on the poplar trees made the landscape look almost French. Down by the oyster pits the waterfront was bustling with activity. Crates full of oysters were being carried to and fro in a way that would baffle outsiders. The mast of the *Vrijbuiter* protruded above the luggers in the distance. Time to set sail and head down the Scheldt Estuary with the ebbing tide."

This sounds straight out of a Hylke Speerstra story about the last of the real skippers, the last men and women to sail cargo ships down the Dutch waterways, propelled only by the wind. He chronicled these stories of a dying world almost a century ago. And in my most romantic moods—which are increasingly rare these days—when people ask me how I make a living, I tell them: I live off the wind. And if you condense this lifestyle down to its essence, you can't argue with that. But there's also the cold world of business, a society that operates by the clock and a government with laws which guarantee that even though you might call yourself *Vrijbuiter*—Freebooter—you'll never be truly free.

The idea behind *Vrijbuiter* was simple. We bought a 120-year-old, flat-bottomed barge that was ripe for the scrapyard. During the first covid lockdown in the Netherlands, we sailed her from Friesland to a warren of islands on the outskirts of Amsterdam to team up with a large group of friends and transform her into a floating haven where the arts, sustainability and great people could all come together. *Vrijbuiter* was to be a catcher of stories because, in the end, stories are all we have. My father once said: no one ever reads out bank statements at a funeral. I don't know where he picked that line up, but he was right.

So off we went, setting sail from Makkum, the old fishing village just below the Afsluitdijk, that 32-kilometre feat of Dutch engineering that protects the country from the North Sea. It was January 4th, 2021, and we had just signed the bill of sale in a notary's office in a stately canalside building in Harlingen. I'd told my wife, Suzan, not to turn down their offer of coffee—notaries are expensive; that coffee came at a steep price. The country was in sleep mode due to the virus. The streets were empty; we were only allowed to sail with a professional crew, so everyone on board had to be certified. We loaded our first cargo: Red De Vloot ("Save the Fleet") craft beer brewed in Harlingen, headed for the big city. Less than an hour after we'd signed on the dotted line, we were out on the open waters. A brisk 6 on the Beaufort scale, heading northeast on lake *IJsselmeer*, we raced past Workum, saw Reid and Cornelie's lighthouse on the dyke in the distance, and discovered that we had no cooking gas on board for making coffee.

At Stavoren, we realised we didn't have any diesel in the tank either. Engineless sailing to Amsterdam! The lake was deserted, the waves rose higher and higher, capricious as lake *IJsselmeer* can be, and there I was, with friends in woollen jumpers and knitted hats, on my own boat with cargo bound for Amsterdam. I stared off into the middle distance, and after a few hours the towers of Enkhuizen appeared on the horizon.

We spent the night there, moored to the floating pontoon. We didn't have to pay any mooring fees—the harbourmaster loved the story of us doing the beer run (a story which, it turned out, had preceded us). In the morning, we set the jib and passed through the lock and out onto Lake Markermeer. The wind had dropped a little, but it was still freezing. We were drinking coffee again; we'd been able to get gas in Enkhuizen. A grey sky melted into grey waters. Our target on shore, the Horse of Marken—the lighthouse on the Marken peninsula— was visible in the distance. After a long, cold day, we turned into the eastern end of the IJ river, still with that stiff northeast wind at our backs. Durgerdam was to our starboard side, Amsterdam sprawling on the port side. We couldn't hear the city with the wind blowing us toward it, but it seemed quieter here too.

We passed through the Oranje Locks. The IJ was deserted. We glided on through the city. Central Station was empty—no one waving or pointing at our boat. By the old timber docks, we turned hard to port and moored smoothly, just as the old skippers must have done a hundred years before us.

But the world doesn't stand still, doesn't wait for people who want to sail by wind alone. We decided to get diesel so we could cruise through Amsterdam at night. There are so many bridges en route that it makes for an arduous journey for masted vessels. It became a pattern for our business in the years that followed—we had to make one compromise after another just to be able to keep sailing. Because a business is what we became: we registered with the Chamber of Commerce, we got company cards, had to do our accounting and started thinking in numbers rather than stories. And time... Before we had the boat we would lose track of time every now and then; with the business we could never find the time to forget the clock.

Today's hectic world is very different from back when the last sailing freighters made their way around the country. It will never again be the way Speerstra described in his stories. Waiting for the wind, anchoring, and waiting for the next tide to come—today there is no time for this. Itineraries have to be planned down to the last minute, and not just for commercial shipping. The strange thing is, Dutch people keep a similarly tight schedule in their 'free' time. Even holidays and day trips are carefully mapped out in advance. The original plan we'd devised with a bunch of friends from maritime college was to sail a flat-bottomed barge around the country without an engine, transporting passengers and cargo, but we soon jettisoned that idea. Even if we had been able to get the exemptions needed to operate a commercial vessel without an engine, the frenzied pace of our society—be it for work or play—makes engineless sailing a non-starter. Just imagine having to tell a private party on a day sail that you have to anchor and wait for the tide to turn before you can continue your journey. People aren't going to accept that.

So what was the best solution? We decided to go electric, but we were already second-guessing whether this was as sustainable as the manufacturers of electric engines would have us believe. After a spate of grant applications and refurbishments, we now cruise electric when we're not sailing. Was it worth it? I'm not so sure. We're part of the rat race again, albeit in the electric category. We have to give talks about how green we are. We're a so-called 'pilot business', but the more time goes by, the more I want to forget about this brave new world and find a way to make our approach to time *itself* more sustainable.

Yes, sailing with an electric engine is cleaner, quieter and cheaper. But if we're serious about transitioning to a more liveable world, above all I think we need to *want* less. Let go of the tight schedules, stop rushing ahead to the next goal. I joined Fairtransport at one point—not necessarily because I believed sailing was the future for cargo shipping, more just to make a statement. I liked the idea of being a cargo shipping company that positions itself in opposition to the cargo shipping industry. Sometimes it feels like selling out to be a part of this world—to be out there all the time, taking up space on crowded waters, just because we're a herald of the future of boating. But it's the stories that emerge as a result of all that rushing around that make sailing the *Vrijbuiter* worth it. To quote my friend, the poet Jan Ducheyne: "life's not all perfect moments, but they do exist, you know—don't just dip your toes in the water, go, go, go!"

So here I am, in the old cabin aboard the *Vrijbuiter*. A Bob Dylan record is playing; a storm is blowing outside; rain is lashing down onto the roof and the loading hatches. The wind turbine at the top of the mast is spinning wildly, then slowing down again. The mussel luggers next to us are tugging against their ropes. As the water rises, so does my despondent mood. When the tide turns, the wind will die down too. I don't need to check the weather report to know that. We're getting a new load of cargo tomorrow—wheat, beer and whisky—and heading for the capital. Through the Volkerak, past the old Hellegat ('Hell Gate') and down the Hollands Diep river, then up the Kil to Puttershoek. Once upon a time, that was a whole town of packet-boat skippers; now, we're the only vessel to occasionally dock in the old ferry harbour. The first time we got there, an old man was standing waiting for us. He'd read in the local paper that we were coming to deliver grain for the millers. He asked whether we understood the tide on the Oude Maas; he began to explain. How he always used to set sail from Hook of Holland. Before we knew it, a new story had begun. For a moment, time came to a standstill. His pipe went out and even though he was an inland skipper, the sea shone in his eyes.

Newtonian Balance: Sailing as Connection with Every Movement

Stevie Hunt

Sailing without an engine has always had a certain mystique to me. What is possible? How is it possible—how do you do it? And significantly: am I able to do it?

The answer to "what is possible?" is, amazingly, "almost anything". An essential part of the possibility is patience. You can't sail against the ebb in Gravesend Reach in a breeze less than about a F2, and you'd struggle to do it with the wind westerly; so, wait until the flood. You can't beat through the lock at Ipswich; so wait for a fair wind, or no wind at all and row or scull. Engineless sailing boats aren't fundamentally limited—the only thing that causes impossibility is a schedule. There are certain things that will never be possible—places where the flow of water is constant in one direction and too strong to ever sail against it, for example; we can either put those places in the same category as mountains, which we happily accept are inaccessible by boat, or innovate something to make it happen: perhaps a system of lines that can somehow haul the vessel against that current. Lots of fun challenges to be had.

The answer to "how is it possible—how do you do it?" is "balance". A sailing boat is a really beautiful study in Newtonian balance; whether for motion or stillness, it's all about balance—equilibrium. Countless elemental forces are acting on the boat all the time; everything you do changes the balance. And there are so many things you can do, so many tools to utilise, to do that. It's all about developing a sense for what the forces are, what they do, and how you can change their balances. Start with the stillness of a mooring. Lean on a mooring rope; that will change the balance and she'll move a little in response to it. Let the mooring ropes go, and she will start to move—sooner or later. The force of the wind starts to overcome the resistance of her hull to the water. Or not. You might have to put a little weight in somewhere. Pushing away from the quay with a boathook perhaps, or in shallow water put a quant pole out; just your weight is enough to alter the balance of forces, and in light airs will move a boat that weighs 160 tonnes. Pulling on a stern rope might draw her head out into a tide that does the rest for you. Pulling on an oar is enough to change balances. Pull on both to make her strike ahead. Pull on one side and she'll turn. Delicate balances. This is before you even touch the helm. The magic starts when you realise that the rudder is only one small part of the orchestra. In open water, sailing in a breeze, you are spoilt because she is quite responsive to the helm. But in light airs or manoeuvring in a tight space you'll often see very clearly that the rudder is such a small part of it all. To get her to bear away in close quarters you might have to ease the mainsheet, perhaps drop the mizzen if you have one; leave the staysail sheeted initially, or if you are coming through a tack keep it backed if you need to turn all the way round—but not for too long, because it will get to the point where all the sails are balanced in a way that means she won't respond to the rudder any more. She'll stop bearing off, and just trudge across the river. Let the staysail draw, and trim it, and she'll start to respond again. When you need her to hold up on to the wind, the mizzen will help. When it gets breezy, you'll need to reduce sail to balance her, to encourage her to go how you need. Put a reef in; that will ease up the helm. Put too many reefs in, and the waves become the dominant force and will stall her. She will wallow uncomfortably, until you put a little more power into the equation. The tide is another tool—recognising that there are six hours of propellant force in the direction you want to go. When there is no wind at all you have an apparent wind as the tide pushes you into the still air. And when the tide turns against you, you can anchor—and all is at rest.

Utilising all these forces is like sorcery. And it certainly feels magical.

And it all feels effortless. Even after the graft of winding up the anchor and setting all the gear; when you stand back, and … She is just sailing. She is moving silently. Effortlessly. Somehow using an engine feels like hard work. The noise is wearing. The smell can be overwhelming. The reliance on people for fuel and spare parts I find stressful. The anxiety of the machine's fragile reliability is palpable. Often someone will say in response to this that the wind isn't reliable. It is reliably unreliable though, and because of that you have countless backup tricks. If you are set up well for sailing without an engine you will have tools to deal with it, and it isn't a problem. Oars for calms, anchors for waiting, drudging or kedging, an understanding of tidal streams and sets, and patience. Engines also skew one's perception of what actually is 'no wind': without an engine you become so much more aware of the subtle movements of powerful air, and how to use air that is moving so slowly as to be otherwise imperceptible. Make smoke to see which way the air is moving; then you manually make the sails the shape they need to be to work. If you heel her over a bit, gravity will help shape them. And sit back and observe. Monitor. And keep playing.

Engines too are instant complacency devices. They encourage you to cut corners, so when they fail, you don't have space or time to sort your backup. It's all-or-nothing; you're in control until you're not. Without the engine it's all a lot more fluid, and you're always on the edge of not being in control, so you always have tricks to ensure you always are on the right side of that line. Safety is often cited as a reason for having an engine. When you don't have one you have to work harder to be safe; therefore you do, therefore you are.

Sailing without an engine draws your consciousness out of yourself: out to the ripples that indicate a breeze; out to other boats whose sailing might indicate an approaching breeze; out to the dark clouds that foretell a squall; out to the movement and shape of the clouds. It draws it out to develop an awareness of the movements of bodies of water, through visual clues. Sets onto shoals and other hazards. Without an engine you need to be better aware of this movement. Spotting the clues, tuning in to everything that is going on around you, every detail.

Sailing for me, then, is sort of meditative. It absorbs my mind completely, and displaces all the nonsense machinations it otherwise favours. I get lost in the vastly detailed processes and the need for constant concentration. I get lost in the movements and the sounds. I get lost in the satisfaction of performing these myriad skills.

An enquirer might rather ask, simply, "why?"

One of the main drivers is my admiration of skill. Skill is among the most beautiful of human qualities, and the skills involved in sailing are very fluid and effectively infinite. You'll never have experienced every possible situation; a lot of the skill lies in responding to unknown, unpractised events. I sail without an engine because I have a deep admiration for others that do. For those that choose to today, and those that have had to historically. For the challenges of it, and the multitudinous skills. There is so much involved in it; it has a complexity like conducting an orchestra, rather than the relatively simple action of forcing a boat along under power. It's an interaction with the world through the boat that builds a complex and fulfilling connection. I find it beautiful, achingly beautiful. It requires utmost concentration and connection with countless skills and tools. It's about attention to detail, and a sense for every movement. Taking clues, information, warnings, with all your senses. It isn't about knowing everything—it's about acknowledging that you don't know everything. You have to acknowledge that because every situation is different, therefore fundamentally you can't know everything. You have to remain open minded and adapt as each situation unfolds. It's about paying very close attention all the time to what is going on, and learning from every moment.

And the answer to the question "am I able to do it?"—well, I'm working on it!

Engineless Sailing:
Rewilding the Soul

Richard Titchener

"**I**f I never sail again, I will remember that evening as the best ever," said Douglas, as he wheeled his bike up the street a few days later. "I was watching through the glasses and thought, oh good, they have made it, as I saw the topsail come down."

He had been bringing his boat back to Maldon as we were returning *Blue Mermaid* to her nearby mooring on the same tide. Earlier, leaving the river Colne, about fifteen miles away, there had been a fickle breeze and eventual calm, so the sweeps had been shipped and our trainees bent to the task assisting the ebb tide in taking us out of the river. We made the tidal gate just before low water and a slight sea breeze wafted us to the mouth of our river, the Blackwater. These two rivers were christened the "last stronghold of sail" by Hervey Benham in his book of the same name in 1948. At that time, sailing barges were still carrying freight, with a sizeable fleet based at Colchester, and Cooks Yard at Maldon was busy maintaining visiting craft. Oyster dredgers and fishermen still plied their trade under sail. Twenty-two years later, in 1970, the last sailing barge to carry cargo finished its circuit, and today, although there are six barges without engines, only token cargoes have been carried. Nevertheless, there are many local ex-working fishing smacks without engines, and it is still possible to feel in tune with Hervey's sentiments.

Our rowers had just experienced drudging backwards with the tide, raising and lowering the anchor manually as the depth changed so it just touched, giving steerage way albeit going backwards. This process harnesses nature to make progress, something denied if an engine takes charge. When weighing anchor there is something very special about feeling the weight change as the anchor breaks out; or how the mate looks at the lead of the chain over the bow, and how the stern is swinging, so as to cast the right way—how each scene in the act needs to be played at just the right moment and in just the right way for the vessel to get under way with a small crew.

The sea breeze failed at the mouth of the river and the hiatus was bridged by the fair tide taking us into the gradient land breeze, which had been there all day. It would be dusk well before high water at the mooring, for this was October, and there seemed every chance we would need to stop and wait for water. But the breeze did not develop into much and by the time we were where we had anticipated stopping, progress was slow and the tide had made enough to keep going.

The jib was dropped, unhanked, folded and bagged, the bowsprit steeved up in the gathering sunset, a magnificent pattern of clouds and light, while all the time the barge was tacked upriver in ever-shallower depths. Now we approached Hillypool, so-called because the tide scours around a bend and creates changing channels and shingle banks at low water where you can walk across, more than a mile below the town quay. Surely soon a leeboard would find the bottom and we would have to wait for water. But no, the flood was almost keeping up with us. The paraffin navigation lights were lit and placed in position, adding an eerie gloom to the gathering shadows each side and aft. Now the course was straight to windward and the available width only three or four lengths. Here is where the arrangement of the barge's gear comes into its own. The mizzen sheets to the rudder, which pulls the sail to windward as the barge tacks. Normally, the foresail then comes into play, held back, until she is safely turned round by a line called a bowline. But here, once round onto a new tack there was barely room to gather way, so that each time, the foresail was dropped and reset when head to wind, to enable the bow to come up. Again, our trainees were experiencing working in harmony with the elements, taking a 27-metre vessel capable of carrying 150 tonnes (or six lorry loads) in just over two metres of water, the hull drawing less than one. The line on the buoy streamed helpfully in the torchlight as we approached, and with a leeboard dropped deliberately in the mud to stop her, and some prompt sail handling, the barge made her mooring with a few inches under her, passing a yacht drawing more water waiting for the tide to make enough to reach her own. As we tidied up full dark came upon us, as did Douglas passing on his way further upriver.

Another day. Another passage, this time with no voyage crew or trainees and just the skipper and mate to bring the barge the thirty-five miles home from the blocks at Pin Mill in Suffolk, where the bottom had been cleaned and antifouled. There is nothing quite like having a clean bottom, especially one that has just been painted. It is one of the bugbears of running a sailing barge that keeping the bottom clean is a regular effort requiring either dry docking at considerable expense or using the traditional method, drying out with the tide on blocks. It is especially important to have a clean bottom without an engine, as your speed and handling are greatly affected by marine growth. If the vessel sits in mud, as *Blue Mermaid* does on her mooring, the antifoul paint soon loses its effectiveness. The sums still work out as the mooring saves on towage, and costs far less than being alongside.

The forecast was for a good breeze, one way of saying it might be too much at times for the topsail, also being a head wind from Walton, about a third of the passage, meaning a substantial addition in distance to be covered compared to how the crow would fly. But it was a fair wind for leaving the blocks with the high water just before midday, and this was achieved without assistance using a spring from the quarter and fetching along the tree-lined shore while the barge boat was lifted, before joining the fairway and calling Ipswich Port Radio. There was enough wind so the topsail was not set until Harwich Harbour, by which time the bowsprit was down, bobstay set up and jib set. The labour involved in all this for two people is considerable, but a handy reminder of the days in trade when two crew would carry up to 150 tonnes of cargo in barges like the original *Blue Mermaid*, which was lost in the Second World War. If you divide the amount of pleasure to be had between the number present, it is difficult to improve on the Thames sailing barge. The legend is that the crew was a man and a boy, and this was often the case during and after the war as only older men and boys were not called up to fight. Prior to that, the larger barges would often have additional crew when economics allowed. In the 1950s and '60s, there was a last generation of young skippers who learnt from their elders and were sorry to see the demise of cargo under sail. It is also worth remembering that wives were known to sail as mate with their husbands, in the same way wartime demonstrated how jobs hitherto regarded as the male preserve could be done by both sexes. One elderly skipper I sailed with many years ago said the war years, when he sailed with his long-lamented wife, were the best of his life.

Now with the topsail set and having alerted Harwich Vessel Traffic Services to our plans, the barge ramped through the harbour and made over eight knots on the electric plotter in the neutral tide across Pennyhole Bay. It was glorious sailing, with inches of freeboard and the rig thrumming in the sunshine. A cloud came over the land by Walton Pier and the topsail was rucked (dropped temporarily) for the squall. The wind direction was such that we almost fetched the Spitway before having to tack inshore for the first time. The topsail reset and, in perfect conditions, the barge ate the miles so it was possible to anchor for a snack at Osea Island and steeve up the bowsprit before reaching the mooring in the early evening.

To sail without an engine is to work in harmony with nature, to rewild the soul at sea. Irrelevant issues are stripped away. When it is ebb tide in the Wallet, it is ebb tide in the Wallet and there is nothing anyone can do about it, as Tom Cunliffe, the well-known sailing author, remarked when supporting the appeal to build the replica *Blue Mermaid*.

Engineless vessels sometimes need a tow, and we certainly rely on this as we do on modern aids, such as the radio, plotter, solar panels and accurate weather forecasts. Sometimes making a passage can take more time. Sometimes it can be as quick as anticipated. In 2023, *Blue Mermaid* delivered ten consignments for a local brewer and did so on time, not without some long days and nights, but with a sense of achievement denied elsewhere. The relationship developed with the vessel in this way is fundamentally different, requiring an affinity for the nuances of balance, and feels quite different from one associated with a powered craft. It helps give an awareness of wind and water which is of benefit to all seafarers, but best gained where it matters most, in sail. This is why generations of our forebears were required to serve time in sail to better understand the effects. Sail training now tends to relate more to character development and teamwork, but there is no reason why the part of our personality in touch with natural forces cannot still have value.

Sailing for the Soul

Mike Jackson

I am fortunate to have had the opportunity to spend time in and on the sea throughout my life, and for me it's always like coming home to a place which makes me feel complete and connected to my essential self. As a child, there were always dinghies of one sort or another around, and safe sailing environments to develop my relationship with the water and the wind. The first boat I called my own was a black and blue Mirror dinghy I christened *Boogaloo*. In her I explored the creeks and byways of Portsmouth Harbour, which at the time was full of rusting warships, sailing boats, tugs, ferries and plenty of other kids in dinghies to race, capsize and generally muck about with. In time I got out into the wider spaces of the Solent strait, and made my first voyages along the coast and over to the Isle of Wight, sometimes sailing solo, sometimes with friends. I have vivid memories of the sense of independence, freedom and pure delight I found in getting my little vessel sailing fast 'on the plane' under spinnaker, tacking upwind effectively, or just being on the water in my own world, leaving the hassles of school life and young teenage angst behind on the land. I went on to sail larger and faster dinghies, then found windsurfing, which came on the scene when I was a teen in the seventies, and offered a new level of speed and full-bodied physical connection with the elements. Around this time, my family started sailing small yachts; then my father built a more substantial yacht in our front garden, which opened up the opportunity to make longer passages along the South coast, and cross-channel excursions to the Channel Islands and the Brittany coast. These early adventures introduced me to the sense of discovery which longer coastal passages offer, the endurance of adverse weather, fatigue and seasickness—which I often suffered from—and the hard won reward of reaching a safe and calm haven after a day, and sometimes a night, at sea. Looking back, it was also the time when I felt closest to my parents as we shared these experiences and their trials and pleasures. Although my Dad did a great job in fitting out his boat (a shallow draft ketch called *Blithe Spirit*), breakages and equipment failure were a normal part of these voyages, and I learned some valuable lessons from him on how to deal with whatever problems emerged with persistence, good humour, and a good enough repair to keep us going. This attitude of self-reliance and having to find our own solution in the absence of any alternative, is a critical part of sailing life, and a valuable foil to the convenience and easiness of land-based life, more so in the internet age where everything is disposable and replaced at the click of a mouse.

During my career in mental health services in the NHS, getting on to the sea has been an essential way for me to cope with the stresses and tribulations of working in a toxic, dysfunctional system with damaged young people who have often experienced terrible things in their lives, which put them at risk of exploitation, self-harm and every kind of social disadvantage. As an adult, I have been able to sail on tall ships, classic yachts, in recent times on my own much loved and very seaworthy yacht, and with the Cirdan Trust in a series of sail-training adventures with young people with psychosis, with whom I work. It has been a joy and a privilege to share my love of sailing with young people who have had none of the opportunities I enjoyed, and to see them learning and appreciating the sea, and the pleasures of sailing for the first time. Being able to share some of the sense of release and freedom I have from untying the ropes which bind me to solid ground, and escape to the space and sanity of the elements, and the simplicity of living on a boat, has been a small way for me to give back and offer something I deeply value to people who need it much more than myself.

Time and space

One of the essential features of being at sea on a sailing boat for me is that it offers a fundamental shift in our experience of time and space. For most of us, in our busy working lives, we are caught in a constant stream of other people, appointments, deadlines, hurry and bustle. On land I have always struggled to catch up and keep up with my own schedules and arrangements with colleagues, patients, friends and family. Once we let go of the shore, we have also to let go of this busy-ness, and abandon ourselves to the slower, eternal rhythms of tide and weather. Sailing is only possible if we accept our relationship to the flow of the wind and tide, which can't be hurried and will not adjust to our habitual notions of time. Sometimes we find ourselves compelled to wait for the wind to change its force or direction before we can reach a destination—and this may involve days in which we just are wherever we are, with any chance of progress and achieve-ment suspended regardless of our supposed plans. To our land-based notion of time, this can feel frustrating and wasteful, but as we adjust to the ocean's ways, it becomes a luxury of release and acceptance. We may have many hours or days of sailing gently, or vigorously, not always in the intended direction, which will not be rushed or changed by our wishes, during which we enter a different consciousness of the constant balance of speed, sail trim, direction, and the endless vista of sea, waves and sky, which is both unchanging and constantly novel. At these times, the elemental presence of the ocean, and its remote-ness and indifference to the concerns of humans, can take on a char-acter which sailors have personified over the centuries in a myriad ways. This profoundly altered experience of time and space can be a vague background awareness, or a powerful and immediate field of awareness, which can be compared to the contemplative states sought in practices such as Zen and mindfulness. In the digital age, getting away from the ubiquitous mobile phone signal, with its social media, email, and constantly available information drained of meaning, is an increasingly difficult to find and valuable opportunity.

Beauty and sensation

The many facets of beauty which we encounter at sea, and their effects on our consciousness and soul, are beyond my words to capture ade-quately, but I will try to describe some of them. The ocean constantly stimulates all of our senses, sometimes forcefully dominating our awareness, more often under the surface of our immediate conscious-ness, but nevertheless contributing to a felt sense of connection with the sea.

It produces an endless stream of sound, from the roaring crash of huge waves of awesome power and weight, to the strangely audible silence of perfectly still water. There is a special magic to falling asleep and waking to the sound of water lapping and bubbling down the side of a moving boat. The wind hums and whistles, and sometimes it howls in the rigging of a sailing boat, evoking nights spent in a harbour's haven listening to the fury of a gale, glad to be safely sheltered from the storm. For me, listening to music at sea can be a special gift, unfiltered by the everyday distractions of land life, bringing an emotional rawness to familiar songs and melodies, and although I shouldn't include this in a section on beauty, I sometimes find myself singing without inhibition, liberated and enriched by the experience.

The bodily, tactile experience of life at sea is similarly rich and varied. We quickly become encrusted with salt, crackling on our skin, which becomes rough and calloused from pulling ropes, heaving the anchor and furling the sails. We are forced to remain in the same small space of the boat, yet we are constantly moving to balance the motion through the waves and the heeling of the boat in the wind, which sometimes threatens to engulf us through capsize or being plunged headlong into the sea. There are periods of delicious stillness at a peaceful anchorage or becalmed and abandoned by the winds, and there are times when the force of the elements is overwhelming and terrifying. Sleep takes on a different quality, broken by changes in the pattern and rhythm of the boat's movement through the water or a change in the sounds of the wind, and our subliminal dreaming consciousness is closer to the surface of our wakefulness, eroding our 'normal' sense of the boundary between reality and imagination.

The experience of eating and drinking at sea is intensified and enhanced by the most important ingredient of any truly excellent meal—a keen appetite, stimulated by massive doses of light and fresh air, and the endless exercise provided by living on a constantly moving vessel. At sea, it can be challenging to prepare even a simple meal, but any sustenance brings an appreciation and enjoyment we rarely feel in our easy land lives where we can reach into the fridge or pop out to the shops at any time. A vivid example of this for me came after a 36-hour upwind passage, much of which I had spent nauseous and vomiting into the sea, leaving me cold to the core, exhausted and flattened. As the conditions eased and I began to faintly recover, my friend brought me a cup of steaming hot lentil and smoked bacon tinned soup, which filled my body with exquisitely delicious flavour, warmth and a flood of restoring energy—one of the most memorable meals of my life. On returning to land a few days later, I watched a cookery programme where the pampered connoisseurs criticised the finer nuances of highly elaborate dishes painstakingly prepared by professional chefs, in an absurd pantomime of the expert appreciation of food, in the absence of natural reality or appetite.

Most obviously, the visual experiences of the sea and the sky when we are away from land, are often intense and numinous. The purity, freshness and beauty of sunrise and sunset at sea can be overwhelming, bringing with them a deep consciousness of the recovery of hope in a new dawn, and the sometimes ominous onset of the long darkness of night without artificial light. The night offers unequalled intensity of stars and moonlight, which we can pass a lifetime on land never seeing. Sometimes this is echoed in the mystical thrill of phosphorescence in the water, dripping from the sides of the vessel, trailing behind in her wake, tracing the outlines of waves, and if we are so blessed, in the trails of unseen cetaceans riding in the bow wave as we surge through the water.

For the seasoned sailor, the boat itself embodies a special beauty, with its harmonic curves—its sheerlines, overhangs and tumblehome— designed to slip and surge through the sea with maximum grace and facility by the accumulated sensibilities of countless generations of boat builders and designers. The curve of a well-trimmed sail in a breeze is a deeply gratifying perfection of aerodynamics, drawing on the flight wings of sea birds to harness the unseen flow of the air mass. Harnessing the wind to provide power and motion, in the context of our self-inflicted fossil fuel burning disaster, only enhances this appreciation.

Life at sea can involve long periods when to a land-based consciousness 'nothing happens', allowing us to drift into reverie or lose ourselves in recollections for hours at a time. In this superficially uneventful context, chance encounters with the exotic fauna of the sea become shockingly intimate, and at times, simply joyful. A pod of dolphins will approach a moving sailing boat and swim with it, sometimes for hours, playing, dancing and apparently exalting in the force produced by the boat moving through the water, like surfers, children in a skatepark, skiers or skydivers. They swim together in a sublime, perfectly synchronised dance, mysteriously and effortlessly interconnected, surfacing and diving together, sometimes leaping and spinning in apparent exaltation of their awe-inspiring physical prowess and skill. In a similar way, the consummate ease with which seabirds, such as guillemots and shearwaters, dip and glide together just above the surface of the water, like figure skaters of the air, is mesmerising. The power and grace of a gannet or a tern, hovering into a plunging dive at terrifying speed, and the barely visible nimble speed of the tiny storm petrel, weaving in amongst huge waves, apparently oblivious to their weight and power.

Companionship and connection

I have done very little solo sailing, so for me sailing has usually been an essentially social experience. Whilst non-sailors might see it as a luxurious activity, a sailing yacht is, in my experience, a small, often cramped place, in which you live without personal space, other than your bunk, rather like camping in a tent or a small caravan. Given that voyages may take many hours or days, you live alongside your companions very intimately, sharing much of the experience moment by moment—including many when nothing much is happening and large periods of uninterrupted time stretch ahead of you. This is characteristic of other kinds of journeying, which many people have observed offer the opportunity for a different type of social interaction. It's neither feasible nor desirable to engage in a continuous conversation for such stretches of time, but interaction tends to spread out and slow down, and there is space for the pleasures of shared, prolonged, comfortable silence. In these circumstances a special kind of intimacy and mutual acceptance is fostered, and you become connected with your companions through the shared experience of the elements and the challenges you encounter together. Over time, the normal social anxieties about self-presentation gradually melt away into a deeper sense of intimacy and connection—something which has been commented on and deeply appreciated by many of the socially excluded and sometimes paranoid young people we have taken sailing. For me it has been an opportunity to deepen and extend my own relationships, and to develop many new and, for me, exciting

54

ones with other seafarers—some much more experienced and wiser than me.

As yet, my sailing experience has been largely coastal and relatively limited compared to the ocean-going adventures of many others. My experiences are superficial in comparison to those who have spent months at sea, sometimes alone, and I refer the interested reader to the many accounts of such voyages for a richer understanding. I hope to extend my own experience in the coming years, but I appreciate that I am privileged and blessed by the opportunities I have had already, and that sailing the ocean on beautiful boats, and sharing this pleasure with others who could benefit from it, has become part of my identity and my aspiration for the future.

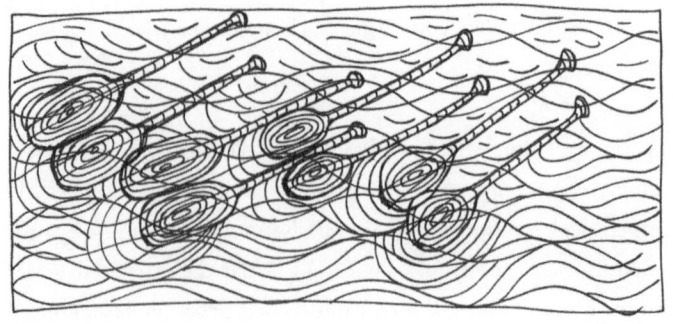

Three Poems

Jessica Taggart Rose

AWAY

nothing like
translucence
sunlight through
white sails' billow
light puff of motion
uninterrupted blues
let tides lift and tug
winds propel until
we make a spec
dissolve to sky
like nothing

WE MOVE WITH THE EARTH'S BREATH

Flutter of jib, long sweep of oar
Rigged to the tides, the weather, the storms
Wind whips the stern, sends spray across bow,
Whistles in rigging, haunting us how
Chimes on the mast, inflates the mainsail
Away, haul away

Sun slants through canvas, glistens on green
Fish leap alongside us, lithe silver in brine
Froth and foam flutter, alight up on deck
Ropes flex and hold, we wash and we wake
Of nature and with her, the give and the take
Away, sail away

Ears to the waves, we trace back their songs
We long for a way

SAILING WITH THESEUS

in a breath
thro the busy scud
good south wind
capes of blue, green shores
I am at rudder, at bow, at mast
we chart from the stars
by salty gales rocked deep
we touch bitten planks
the ship remains the same

windless
when only the light seeped
when nothing happened but the horizon

This cento is composed from the following source poems:
Alfred Noyes, "Immortal Sails"; Coleridge, "Fragment 1" and
"Rime of the Ancient Mariner"; Helene Vacaresco, "Black Sails";
Rachel Zucker, "When All Hands Were Called to Make Sail";
Judith Minty, "Sailing by Stars"; Frances M. Frost, "Legend of Sail
Rock"; Edwin Morgan, "Sailing or Drowning"; Christine Garren,
"Ghost Ship"; Plutarch, *Vita Thesei*; and Adam Zagajewski,
"Great Ships".

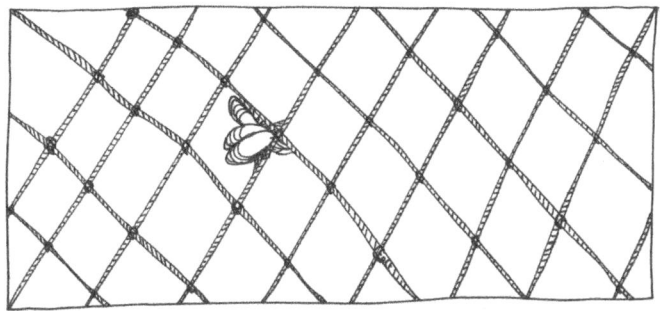

Sing Out When Turns

Emma Rault

By the time we came out of lockdown, I was half-crazed. My wife and I had moved across LA just before the pandemic hit, to be nearer the ocean in a place with more of a small-town feel, where our neighbours weren't all haughty twentysomethings building their Instagram brands. Somewhere we could forge community. Instead, we'd spent our first year in San Pedro at home, having occasional shouted, socially distanced conversations with our new neighbours from the balcony: about the evil yellow wildfire smoke that blew south from San Francisco, about the National Guard-mandated curfew, about the insurrection. About this country, where I'd barely put down my suitcases—I was still on a conditional green card at the time—and which seemed to be breaking bit by bit.

In hindsight, I wish I could say I was braver, that I went out into the world in my cloth mask to document the times. But I was too frightened, too filled with distrust as the US authorities continued to downplay the situation while we watched helicopter footage of morgue trucks crowding New York City streets. So we locked way down, taking advantage of our remote jobs to ride it out at home. By the time we re-emerged, in the spring of 2021, I'd forgotten how to be with people. I felt skinless and skittish, desperate for company, yet surprised to be hounded by a paranoia I hadn't felt since adolescence, my brain somehow equating social distancing with the experience of being shunned. I'd walk into a store, a bar, and think *everybody here hates me*. I found myself avoiding people's eyes.

It was around this time that I learned about the tall ships. When I mentioned I'd lived on a canal boat in Britain, a neighbour asked, "Oh, have you thought about crewing on the brigantines?"

I'd seen them on my lockdown walks down by the waterfront: two towering behemoths with intricate webs of rope and cream-coloured sails, throwbacks to the golden age of seafaring. I had assumed they were like the *Cutty Sark* in London—just for display. It turned out they were owned by a non-profit organisation whose mission was to teach young people from the LA area how to sail. The brigantines were two-masted, 110-foot, wood-hull sailing vessels built to resemble 19th-century windjammers, each with a total of thirteen sails. Pirate ships. That's how people tended to think of them. Even with a group of kids there to help, they took at least six, ideally eight, crew members to sail, so there was a constant need for volunteer deckhands to supplement the full-time liveaboards—no prior sailing experience needed.

Groucho Marx famously said, "I don't want to belong to any club that will accept me as a member." I've always felt the opposite: that being let in is no small thing at all. Over the years, I've joked about being the anti-Groucho Marx: I'll go almost anywhere that is willing to have me. So the next week, in a pair of $15 non-slip deck shoes from Target—in case the new hobby doesn't stick, I thought—I walked down to the tumbledown old waterfront, past the whale-watching ticket booth and the fish market restaurant that sat rotting on its stilts awaiting gentrification, and slipped through a crack in the chicken-wire fence to the dock.

✳

San Pedro has a strange waterfront. Originally a sprawling network of marshes and mudflats, it was drastically reconfigured around the turn of the century by LA's captains of industry. They dynamited natural islands and ploughed up Indigenous shell mounds from the Gabrielino-Tongva people to pave the way for what is now the largest container port in North America. Across the main channel that runs along the eastern end of town out to sea, there are miles and miles of shipping containers stacked like LEGO blocks; shining seas of Toyotas freshly arrived from Japan.

Once home to Navy shipyards, tuna canneries and dive bars, San Pedro prides itself on being a 'port town, not a beach town', different from the sleeker seaside communities—Redondo Beach, Malibu, Santa Monica—along LA's western coastline. Its unofficial mascot is a three-eyed mutant fish, originally a mural by local artist Dave Butkus, a tongue-in-cheek reference to the notoriously polluted waters. (There is a massive toxic dump site about ten miles off the coast. Initially the 27,000 barrels were believed to contain DDT. This year, it became apparent the DDT had been dumped straight into the ocean; the barrels may in fact contain low-level radioactive waste.)

I'd learned that Peeedro, as locals called it—never 'Pay-dro'—was like that: acerbic, full of bravado, an underdog wearing its battle scars with pride. But speculators were catching on, trying to commodify the working waterfront as 'industrial chic'. The sailor dives had been razed back in the '70s; the fish market, the last holdout from a folksy shopping village called Ports O' Call, was next, to make way for giant warehouses with food courts in them dubbed 'West Harbor'. There were plans for a members-only dog park.

＊

Before I came to LA, I'd spent three years living on a narrowboat as part of the UK's itinerant boating community, who make their home on the remnants of the Victorian canal system that fuelled the Industrial Revolution. I'd mentioned it when I applied to volunteer on the tall ships to prove that I wasn't *completely* clueless, but the truth was that stepping aboard one of these majestic vessels, my previous boating experience felt flimsy and remote. The jargon alone was completely new: *clews* and *bunts*, *booms* and *yards*, *halyards* and *downhauls*. I'd study the instructional diagram in my logbook at home, trying to memorise which lines—always 'lines', never ropes—led to which sails, reciting the order of the square sails a hundred times in my mind (from top to bottom: t'gallant, upper, lower, course) but on the boat, in confusing 3D, I couldn't remember any of it. In the beginning, I felt most at home down in the engine room, next to that great throbbing heart which for years, back in England, had been the pulse of home.

The people on board seemed different than back in the UK, too. Tall ships attracted daredevils. There were crew members who never took their harness off, rigging knife clipped onto their belt, always ready to go aloft, preferably while the boat was underway. ('Going aloft' meant climbing to the top of the mast and then dangling up there to furl the square sails or free a fouled line. Early on, in what I can only describe as the world's worst attempt to reassure myself, I googled "going aloft dying", which effectively guaranteed I would *not* be doing the climb.)

But there were parallels. Like the boat-dwellers on Britain's canals, they were misfits, free people. Gary, the old captain with his cracked bare feet and faithful Great Dane (one eye white, one black) permanently in tow; first mate Grizz, with his bushy beard and neo-Pagan knuckle tattoos; Chelsea, with her fantasy novels and a homemade T-shirt that said, "Has Someone Talked to You About Your Solarpunk Future?" Many of the crew were young, sometimes just out of college, sometimes just there for the season—but others stayed for years, rotating between tall ships on both coasts and in the Great Lakes region, or alternating between the boats and other seasonal work, like the train hoppers of the 1920s. They seemed to be looking for a different way of being in America, for community, freedom from the capitalist grind. I listened in horror as they one-upped each other with tales of how they'd managed horrendous injuries without health insurance, and felt a fierce envy as they talked about Renaissance fairs and cannon battles. My life, by comparison, seemed safe and staid and old.

I was often the only part-timer on one-day trips, or 'day sails'; being self-employed gave me a flexibility that not many volunteers had during the week. The full-time liveaboards weren't easy to be around at first. I liked Jonah instantly, with his Baphomet coffee mug and sly, goat-like face, but he never talked, and as so often in my life, I took reticence to be a targeted rejection of me personally. It took me a year, and someone else ribbing him about it, to realise he was like that with everyone. As a group, they had the kind of effortless intimacy with each other that is born of constant closeness: the captains got a cabin of their own, but all of the deckhands slept in tiered bunks on either side of C compartment. Later, I'd feel enormously flattered when they welcomed me into their social world; until then, I found it totally intimidating.

And there were the kids, of course. On every sail, we had around thirty middle-schoolers or high-schoolers on board—so loud, so many—kids who descended on the boats like a storm. At first, intimidated by their rowdiness, I hid in the background, stowing backpacks below deck before setting sail, coiling and hanging lines once we were underway. Soon, I was assigned the task of taking groups out onto the netting that hung underneath the bowsprit, the long spar that protruded like the nose of a swordfish from the ship's prow. They would get into safety harnesses, clip their carabiners onto metal lines that ran along either side of the bowsprit, and begin to make their way out. For the kids, this was usually the scariest part—so many shrieks of "I'm gonna die! I'm gonna die! No, I'm *definitely* gonna die." But when they got there, they would sit in the sun, either straddling the bowsprit or reclining, hammock-style, in the netting below, listening to the sound of the bow scything forward through the waves. That was, without fail, the absolute best part of their day.

I was amazed to see how gentle they were with each other—talking one another through the practical steps, encouraging the more fearful to be brave. I hadn't been around teens since I'd been one myself, and my own adolescence had been socially brutal. I felt a combination of pangs and wonder, seeing how different things might have been. At the same time, I felt keenly aware of the things I'd never had to deal with. I winced when students referred to their active shooter drills; bit my tongue listening to teens from our local high school map out careers in the army as their ticket out of town.

The two boats each fostered their own distinct cultures: one was more touchy-feely, more cliquey, more laissez-faire; on the other, they tended to be more by-the-book. I tried to split my time equally between both, but in my first months, I always seemed to end up on the latter one, crewing with James, a gentle boy with a flax-blond moustache, and Nora, who'd grown up in Oman and had to deal with serious reverse culture shock coming back to the US for college. The two of them taught me what I needed to know, sometimes in surprising ways—when I told Nora about my day job and she asked, "Do you like being a translator?" for the first time I realised I was no longer sure of the answer.

And they taught me to look at the ocean. The day sails involved teaching students about the ocean in hands-on marine biology lessons, using creatures retrieved from a lobster trap we'd pulled up at the dock and transferred to Tupperware. Here was a whole new category of undulating life I'd never seen before: abalone, a mollusk that parted its shells to reveal a bright pink softness, strangely womblike, which propelled itself by kicking furiously through the water; sea squirts, globs of jelly that grew in viscous mats on rocks and, if squeezed gently, would spurt out a jet of the seawater from which they drew their plankton diet. The braille of barnacles growing on mussel shells— these were all beings I'd never noticed before, or hadn't consciously registered as animate.

I'd grown up with the North Sea and the Atlantic, the coastlines of the Netherlands, where I lived, and France, where my ancestors came from and to where my family still gravitated on vacations. It was part of why I had a hard time connecting with the Pacific Ocean when I first moved to LA. I thought of myself as a grey sea kind of person, a roiling sea (if seen from the safety of the shore) to mirror my inner angst. The Pacific, like the sunny weather, seemed too placid, too 'feel good'. Yet now I realised how little I truly knew about living with the ocean. When Captain Gary was talking to a school group about how sailing was a much more sustainable option in the climate change era, it suddenly hit me how oblivious I'd been to the way my own relationship with the water fit into a wider web of life. On the canal, chugging along with my gasoline Honda, I'd never really considered the environmental impact of this sort of boating lifestyle. I guess I thought that if this was eventually going to be phased out, that was good for 'us'—i.e., humans. It changed things to carefully peel a sea star's tube feet off a bucket at the end of the afternoon and return him to his home. As that first sailing summer turned into fall and winter, I started going down to the tide pools in the afternoons, watching entire universes sway and scuttle in tiny dips of coastal rock. This ocean was so much more than backdrop or metaphor.

Like my canal boat, being on the tall ships made me pay closer attention to the land too. Gliding past the fish market and the fuel dock, we'd pass the long pink building on piles where sea lions would circle as the fishing boats unloaded their catches, their hoarse barks echoing in the space between water and concrete. I realised that, some nights, I could hear their *urk urk urk* from up on the hill where we lived, along with the assertive cry of the lighthouse, that great green blinking eye at the end of the breakwater. To the west there was the slope of San Pedro Hill, the highest point on the Palos Verdes Peninsula. Seen from the water, it all looked somehow smaller and yet more momentous at the same time. Cliffs that had formed millions of years ago, dotted with the flickering of our little lives.

Time also felt different on the water. Going to Dana Point by car, a nearby seaside town in Orange County, involved an inland route barrelling for an hour down a ten-lane freeway. Going there on the tall ships took objectively longer—five times as long, in fact—but it felt like those hours stretched and elongated into days. During 2020, I'd picked up a fierce doomscrolling habit, fracturing my mind and my days into tiny, jagged pieces. Beyond the breakwater there was no signal, just a surging continuum of blue and the demands of the moment keeping you in place.

In early spring, a few hours into my first overnight voyage to Dana Point, a beautiful gay man named Mark, with formidable lamb chop sideburns, pulled some string out of his pocket and asked me, "Have you ever tied a bowline knot?"

I sat down next to him, wondering when was the last time I'd sat with someone to learn something simple and hands-on, without the aid of the internet? I couldn't even remember. I watched the deft movements of his fingers, his knuckle tattoos that spelled out HOLD FAST. "The rabbit goes into the hole ... around the tree ... back into the hole." As I clumsily copied him, repeating the mnemonic out loud, I observed with wonder my mind slowing to something resembling peace.

The weird thing was, half the time I felt like I didn't want to be sailing at all. I'd feel seasick or cold (it took me months to master dressing in layers) or impatient. I've always had a tendency to see the practical as a distraction from the cerebral, left over from a childhood of being book-smart and physically inept. Often, I'd feel myself bristling at sailing's endless succession of chores, especially the prospect of having to furl the sails once back in port, a process of fighting with stiff Dacron and fraying lines, exhausted and ravenously hungry, to the soundtrack of the fish market's relentless mariachi. But somewhere out at sea, no matter how long or short the trip, there was always a point where something inside me would loosen. More than anything, it was this feeling that kept me coming back.

For me, the tall ships were also an object lesson in American culture, in all its guises and with all its contradictions. There was Colt, for instance, the first mate who'd grown up on a ranch and had bicep tattoos of a bull skull and a revolver—the first person I met who didn't just ape the trappings of Western style, but who actually *was* a cowboy. (He had a cowboy's bravado, complete with a resolute indifference to the then still-in-place masking mandate, but surprised and charmed me at an event by being a painfully shy public speaker.) And there was Orion, with his chipped nail polish and embroidered flourishes sewn onto his crew hoodies, who taught me the proper way to fold an American flag—we usually flew one at the top of the mast, and that particular day had to change it out for a less tattered specimen—concluding his tutelage with the words, "And that's how it's done," and then a leaned-in, half-whispered, "But I don't give a fuck."

Riding to an event with two middle-aged sailors, I made an off-hand comment about America's relationship with firearms only to discover, to my surprise, that I was in a car with two gun owners. (By their own accounts, "to shoot at cans in the desert", and for bed-side-drawer safety—although they both admitted that they weren't sure they were skilled enough to actually use a gun in self-defence, if it came to it.) I was strangely grateful for moments like these, encounters with genuine difference that challenged my facile, foregone conclusions, my ideas about Americans who did this or believed that.

Summer came around again; summer camp season started. This meant a succession of trips to Catalina Island—or "the island", as local boaters simply called it. Once a favoured getaway for Hollywood stars—it was where Natalie Wood had her drowning accident—it was the landmass directly across from San Pedro, just twenty-two nautical miles away. On clear days, it felt like you could reach out and touch it from the mainland, but a ferry to Avalon—the touristy main town, with its pastel cottages and people riding around in golf carts— was a prohibitive $70 return trip.

The tall ships, on the other hand, could go anytime and anchor anywhere. It felt magical to drop anchor off Two Harbors—a tiny town at the isthmus, just an inn, a campground, a restaurant and some housing for seasonal workers—and whizz over in our small inflatable. And at the docks it was the granddaughter of the man who'd started our organisation who caught our line, tan and confident in chino shorts, working for the local Harbor Department.

By now, I was less clueless. I'd learned the rhythms of a voyage, working my way forward from the main to the jibs as we set the sails, increasingly finding myself in the right place at the right time rather than circling confusedly or getting in the way. When we braced the square sails—turned them to face the wind—you had to either loosen a set of lines or pull on them, depending on whether you were on port or starboard. Before, I always had to ask a crew member which one I was supposed to do; now, when the first mate called out "Let go and haul," I just knew.

On the summer camps, I learned more about American culture. I learned what American kids eat, helping to prepare industrial-size vats of gluey spaghetti served with 'Texas toast' (sliced garlic bread from the freezer aisle); ready-bake cinnamon rolls from foil-and-cardboard tubes that opened with a loud pop. Even more than the day sails, the summer camps were where worlds collided. People who were largely strangers to each other got thrown together for five days to figure things out. Sometimes, it was painful to see the usual inequities becoming apparent, even here. The one time we had a group from a fancy L A private school, it was striking how much more bubbly, confident and relaxed they were than the students from the public school system we got on our day sails. Here were kids who waxed lyrical about buying vintage first-edition Washington Irving novels in London; who, in virtually the same breath, talked about biodynamic farming and the differences between British, Spanish and Portuguese imperialism. Kids who were dizzyingly, unabashedly smart, but who were also getting every opportunity to cultivate their interests. It seemed patently unfair: there were kids who showed up to the boats hungry, who'd never even seen the ocean before, didn't know what a heron was; and then there were kids who got to go antiquarian book shopping halfway across the world.

On another summer camp, Captain Carolyn found a non-binary teen crying in their bunk after being aggressively questioned about their gender by a group of homeschooled Christian girls. It was the same kid—witty, introspective, fiercely intelligent—whose mom we had to call after the voyage when we discovered they'd left their Prozac on board. Why did it have to be *them* with the social strife and the Prozac prescription—even now, even in L A? Why is it always us, struggling to stay on an even keel, to be accepted for who we are?

At other times, though, worlds collided in surprising and beautiful ways. In late summer, we hosted a group of homeschooled Mormon kids from Utah, with a few parent chaperones. At the time, I was involved in a local political battle and seemed to be fielding an endless succession of stressful phone calls. On our way out of the harbour, hiding down in the galley—discreetly, I thought—I had to have a particularly unpleasant conversation with the editor of a local magazine who had printed some damaging and inaccurate information about me.

When I was recomposing myself on deck afterwards, one of the parents, a soft-spoken man with a long, dark beard, came up to me and asked, "Emma, have you seen the new *Star Trek* series?"

I shook my head.

"There's a character named Sulu. He has this very calm, gentle way about him, but when you cross him, he's a force to be reckoned with. I overheard you on the phone earlier. You remind me of him."

I was taken aback, because that wasn't how I thought of myself at all: I always saw myself as someone who struggled to assert boundaries. When I got angry, I felt like I just came across as cornered and shrill. Later that day, I looked the character up on my phone and discovered that in the new *Star Trek*, Sulu was gay. I wasn't sure if that was part of why the comparison had occurred to him, but I felt tremendously flattered to be seen in this way—likened to a character who was queer, empowered, equanimous—and by a Mormon man, no less, someone I might have expected to be judgmental towards me. Through the months that followed, as I continued to be maligned by property developers and argue with local politicians, I carried the compliment with me like a talisman.

Over the course of that week, I watched rapport gently and gradually build between the Mormons and gay, non-binary and Pagan crew members, people from communities generally presumed to be at odds with each other. (One night Jojo—who had a "THEY/THEM" sticker prominently on their HydroFlask—recalled how during that afternoon's swim, a student had come paddling up and blurted out, "I like your water bottle," before diving under and swimming away.) Time and again, these moments of connection—quicksilver, delicate, a lattice of sunlight on water.

Sometimes, I wished the non-profit was more overt about how it positioned itself. We didn't fly a Pride flag in June. And as I began to learn more about California's history, I noticed how little we reflected on what tall ships represented in that context. For some Indigenous people, they symbolised dark things, their arrival on the horizon marking the start of cataclysmic loss and change. At the same time, there was something to be said for steering clear of sloganeering and position statements and simply creating a space where conversations about these kinds of topics could unfold naturally.

Time and again, the tall ships proved me wrong—about other people, about myself, about things I thought I didn't want or wasn't capable of. I discovered you can make do with so much less than you think you need—that you can eat with relish mere feet from where someone has just projectile-vomited. That eaten outside, "on the hook" (at anchor), gluey spaghetti and Texas toast taste fantastic.

I always thought snorkelling wasn't for me—the wetsuit, the awkward plastic mouthpiece (like being at the dentist!), the frigid water of the Pacific—but when another deckhand talked me into it, at Emerald Bay on the north-western tip of the island, I almost cried: undulating fronds of seaweed, blue flowers, electric orange slivers of Garibaldi fish. Unearthly and tentacular vegetation: furry mosses stirred up by the water, kelp combed by the current. I thought about that line from a Gerald Manley Hopkins poem, about "the dearest freshness deep down things", and was struck, like I had been at the tide pools, by how a place I'd never paid attention to before could be so brilliantly alive.

The lexicon of sailing, so foreign at first, gradually lodged itself in my mouth. There was something deeply reassuring about the pattern of call and response. You always had to respond to commands so that the other person knew you'd heard them, repeating phrases that you knew had rung out for hundreds of years. As I'd become more familiar with how the sails worked, I'd come to understand that everything was connected. You couldn't take up slack on one line until someone else had secured the opposing line. You had to do your part so someone else could do theirs. On the boats, in that context, the phrase to let someone know you were ready so they could proceed was "Sing out when turns". ("Turns" meant two turns of the line wrapped around the pin.) Of all the commands, it was that one I fixated on for some reason. Its lyricism (*sing* out), its shorthand, the way it spoke to being part of a bigger whole—knowing what was needed of you. Knowing you were needed.

✳

After voyages, the language of sailing would drift through my head like songs. *Turns halyard. Pass headsails. Anchor's on the cat.* Back on land, I'd feel homesick for the boat. I'd miss the constant burble of the ship radio poking through my sleep (*This is United States Coast Guard, Sector San Diego, United States Coast Guard, Sector San Diego...*); the unearthly clarity of the sky at 4am, during the hour of night watch each of us had to complete when we were at anchor. I'd miss the giddy feeling that we were getting away with something: purple-haired, unwashed, barefoot like wild things, we seemed so young, it was hard to believe we were allowed to take this giant boat out to sea, entrusted with, as Carolyn's coffee mug read, "Keeping the Small Humans Alive".

But there was something lovely, too, about the pattern of going and coming back; about the interstices between journeys, when I got to hang out with the crew in Building G (where they had the shore luxuries of plumbing, a ping-pong table, a widescreen TV) and, for the first time, got to be the settled friend, the one who was more in the know about the minutiae of life on land. The liveaboards only had a vague sense of the goings-on in San Pedro, which could make hanging out with them a welcome respite from the debates that were raging locally. (At an event, listening to a local bigwig bemoan the imminent loss of the fish market to the forces of change, one crew member quizzically noted, "If they like it so much, why don't they just keep it?")

However idyllic much of this may sound, I spent much of the sailing season angry with myself. I constantly felt I was failing, wasn't learning fast enough, wasn't doing enough, bonding with the kids enough, making myself visible enough. I felt stuck in awkward transition—I wasn't really a sailor, but I was also still too guarded and depressed to truly show up as a person.

And much of the time, the world felt broken. The forests were bone dry and dangerous; the ocean we loved was littered with DDT. On the final night of our voyages, we'd anchor off Long Beach, by the four manmade islands where futuristic fake towers disguised oil rigs. Every time I saw them, I'd feel angry they existed at all. Amid all of that, was sailing really the best way to be spending my time? In those moments, it felt banal, pointless. What would my epitaph say? "She Stood Here, She Pulled Some Lines"?

But there was a moment on one of the last voyages of the season, when I snuck below deck for a cat nap and looked around. I took in the hand-drawn "Fair Winds and Following Seas" postcard tacked to the wall; the tropical fish and "No Music, No Life" stickers on the top starboard bunk; the handmade dreamcatcher of twigs and feathers, string and a pinecone. All at once, I was overcome by a thought I've often had in community settings: I may not be the most skilful pair of hands, but I will love all this with the closest attention I can muster.

And there was another moment, not long after, waking up on the final morning of a voyage—yes, off those hated Long Beach oil islands—and stumbling upstairs to find the others had let me sleep in; we were already underway. There were curls of fog on the water, the sun hung sleepy and low, and Aaron—one of our British crew members—wordlessly pressed a mug of Yorkshire breakfast tea into my hand. I took a sip, tasted my previous boating life on the canals, saw the present through the groggy haze of a child who's drifted off on the sofa at a family party. I felt at home.

All through that summer and beyond, whenever the world felt impossible, when I felt choked by fear—I'd go down to the boats. I'd stand there, I'd pull some lines. And something would shift.

Sailing Without an Engine:
Lessons in Life Skills

Jude Brickhill

We glide into the anchorage, under cliffs looming black against the night sky, as the dew-damp sails lift idly in the fading breath of wind and the leadswoman's call charts the seabed below us. The rattle of the chain as the anchor goes down feels unnaturally loud and final. We are two days late and below decks is a mess of salty bedding and spilt stew. But we are here. Present in mind and body.

I have been sailing for over fifty years, very rarely in a boat with an engine, and I must admit that I never thought of engineless sailing as a 'thing'. In my experience there's such a world of difference between the two that it seems strange to define one in terms of the lack of the other.

Sailing without an engine never seemed particularly remarkable. I learned to sail in small racing dinghies, then graduated to a 25-foot Bermudan rigged fin keeler whose engine, a long shaft Seagull outboard, never worked so was jettisoned early on. When we came to Cornwall, we were looking for a sailing home for our growing family and had just discovered the wonder and delight of the local traditional working boats when we found the 1911 mackerel drifter *Guide Me*. She had been built just before the advent of engines, and when we restored her, we wanted to share what we could of the sailing experience of those hardy fishermen, whose vessel we found so beautiful and strangely well suited to our very different times and life style.

I loved the sense of purpose that these working boats shared, all with specific rigs and hull shapes to match exactly the demands of their various tasks—crabbers, long liners, trawlers, pilot cutters, cargo boats— in the seas and weather, the mud and rock, of their own localities. And what the men who sailed those Cornish mackerel drifters did, I found awesome. In good weather and bad, they sailed, or rowed or warped out of harbour on the tide, out to the fishing grounds off Cornwall and beyond, where they set their nets and lowered the foremast to lie easier to the mizzen. When they had hauled the catch aboard into the fish hold, they stowed the nets, hoisted the mast again and cracked on sail to catch the tide and be first to the fishmonger's slab.

We weren't about to re-enact all that, but there were characteristics to these craft that dovetailed surprisingly well with what we had in mind. We were a young family wanting to adventure out across the world's oceans and here was a vessel, built to handle the changeable weather and demanding seas around the British coasts, a fast, sea-kindly, load-bearing hull with a rig both simple and cheap, albeit labour intensive.

She was low tech, made of tarred and oiled wood secured with iron nails, yet perfectly designed to carry precious cargoes—fish or family—over rough seas and in and out of coastal nooks and crannies more challenging than any I'd ever imagined, and solely under sail. The fact that she had been built and worked without an engine meant that the boat was capable and it was up to us to learn how to handle her unfamiliar rig to get the best out of her, as the fishermen had before the 'iron topsail' swept all before it.

With engines came the comforting reassurance of a super power which could override tides and contrary or fickle winds, deliver cargoes to a prearranged schedule and use a fraction of the labour required for sailing. It brought a sense of control and certainty that transformed the fishing and shipping industry and left sailing to decline into the domain of small traditional fleets, like the Falmouth oyster dredgers, and the leisure industry. Even there, engines are now deemed a necessary and welcome addition to a vessel's propulsion, with their promises of superhuman power over the elements, the ability to save time and effort, and ensure, or at least attempt, control of the vessel. They seem to make everything so much easier and simpler than in the days of sail alone, and in many ways, they do.

But there is an important caveat to this augmentation of our power. Not only are engines dependent on fossil fuels, with all their harmful impacts on our planet, but, in everything we have gained from them, there is little appreciation of what we have lost. Sailing without the option of an engine creates ideal conditions for learning some invaluable life skills that stand you in good stead whatever you may be doing.

For a start, you have to pay close attention to what is going on around you because, under sail, you have no brakes, no handy reverse gear to get you out of a tight spot. You have no choice but to co-operate with the forces at work, the strength of the wind, the momentum of the boat, the direction of the tide. You need these to work with you, not against you, and the only persuasion you have is in the set of the sails and the angle of the rudder, all powered by human effort and intention and informed by your observation and experience. You have to make snap decisions, assessing risks to the best of your knowledge and ability, and take responsibility for your actions because a mistake can mean damage or worse. You learn to do what has to be done, let go a sheet, tail on a halyard, take a turn on the pump as the boat tacks, no matter what, because, as Forester's *Hornblower* said, "The ship comes first."

With practice, you learn to trust your judgement, to focus on the detail of the task in hand yet remain aware of the peripheries and to recognise the supreme importance of co-operation and teamwork. No matter your role, whether fore deck, aft deck, navigator, helm, cook or photographer, you are part of a crew, acting together with a shared purpose in which everyone's contribution is valuable, part of an enterprise that involves working with elements far more powerful than you, and that is a very humbling realisation. There is no room for complacency or arrogance for the sea will detect any oversights or assumptions. When the wind dies, you learn patience and the acceptance of a situation beyond your control, apparently endless yet changing all the time, so there is no let up in the need to be present that might seem more urgent in a breeze. You discipline yourself to rest when you are off watch, to pace yourself, because your contribution may be needed at any moment, and it matters.

In being so relentlessly present you make some wonderful discoveries. There is a strange freedom in being immersed in the moment, not constrained at all, reaching from the deck under your feet, to the phosphorescent bow wave and stretching as far as the stars, held in a timeless space that echoes to the rhythm of the ocean. Using an engine diverts your attention to the time-driven world, eclipsing the sense of your own agency and potential, and blunting that edge of clarity that teaches you the essential skill of sailing, of being a part of the whole force field through which our seaborne lives are moving.

I feel sailing is about so much more than getting from A to B. Every voyage is uncertain and no landfall is the same, and it is that very uncertainty that hones the blade of our alertness. It enables us to deal with the unexpected with fluidity, balance and stamina, and to experience the challenge and exhilaration of finding a trust in something greater than our own efforts. We learn humility at the realisation of our insignificance in the immensity of the environment, and awe and respect for the natural forces around us. Flexibility, resilience and balance, along with appreciation and gratitude for each safe passage, each dawn, however grey, each dolphin, each harbour light—these are useful life skills in our fast-changing world, as are risk assessment, ingenuity and problem solving on the fly. Sailing without an engine is far from the primitive and irrelevant indulgence that it is often painted to be. To my mind, there is no finer way of celebrating the lives and expertise of our forebears than by using what they teach us to fully inhabit the present in a way that honours and protects the future of our infinitely precious and glorious world.

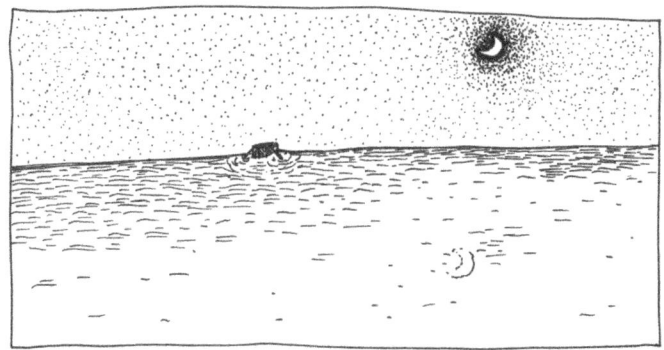

Guide Me

Jude Brickhill,
set to music by *Pat Hobden*

She was only a beat up fisher lass, but she stole my heart away,
Beached like a whale in the Fareham mud that long ago
    evening in May.
Through the barnacled slime, the tingles and rust, her lines shone
    fair and true,
A sailing lugger of years gone by from the far western port of Looe.
And you will guide me onward, our voyage not near done,
Though storm and tempest and wild winds blow, you'll guide me
    safely home.
She's an elegant lady, this old fisher lass, her bulwarks now
    gleaming with oil,
Hull glistening with tar, she's carried us far, powered by love's
    family toil

And she'll take us there if we choose to go, with joy in her heart
    like a foal,
For hauling up sails and dancing round decks is labour that's fit
    for the soul.
And you will guide me onward, our voyage not near done.
Though storm and tempest and wild winds blow, you'll guide me
    safely home.
She's a gorgeous, re-born fisher lass, though these days the fishing's
    for dinner.
In summer we sail, for Brittany bound, in winter she sleeps
    in the river.
From the port of Looe and Helford's fine shore, 'cross the world
    our fair lady has roamed
At her family's side, for many a tide, now Gweek calls our
    fisher lass home.
And you will guide me onward, our voyage not near done
Though storm and tempest and wild winds blow, you'll guide
    me safely home.

Hope Adrift: Shipwreck, Search and Rescue

COMMEMORATING THE 200TH
ANNIVERSARY OF THE RLNI AND KNRM:
SAVING LIVES AT SEA FOR 200 YEARS

Artur C. Jaschke

"Man's Life in this world seems to be
Like the drift of a ship on a wintry sea;
A calm to-day; to-morrow a storm;
A sunset fair: then a troubled morn.
Happy the man whose notion tends
To take whatever the good Lord sends.
In other lands we meet kind friends
When Fate compels us there to roam;

But the dearest friends the good Lord sends

Are friends we meet when we come home.

Home again! Home again! From a foreign shore

And oh! It fills my heart with joy

To see those friends once more."

— Excerpt from Captain Job Barbour's *Forty-Eight Days Adrift*

The words of relief and hope of a captain, who has been faced with one of the greatest challenges sailing can bring: a dismasted ship, a frightened crew, and the dire prospects of never returning back home.

Hope, however, can be a dangerous mistress. While sailing far away from land, we have only ourselves to rely on when solving the problems that occur, day in day out. Yet, as we move closer to shore, encountering more turbulent air currents, we are filled with the hope that regardless of the difficulties ahead we will be safe. This feeling of safety, however, can be an illusion, dependant on the courage of women and men who risk their lives to save us, when there is no real prospect of hope, when we drift dismasted towards the jagged cliffs of what was once a safe haven. Countless ships and their crew have been denied the safety of the shore, their ships stranded on sandbanks or shattered against cliffs during a violent storm.

In such circumstances, we can only hope that we will survive. Yet, what is hope? While hope seems to have enabling functions, keeping us focused on a better outcome than the reality of the situation within which we find ourselves, it also precludes a more attainable positive future through a disinclination to any further risk taking. In order to believe that our situation will change, that a certain state of reality will happen, we are trusting in our own hopeful probabilities, fuelled by our experience, beliefs or the magnitude of what we think we know (i.e., our ignorance).

"Hope ... is the great Wheel, or rather Weight that moves Man to all Actions and Undertakings. The Plough-man Ploughs in Hope; and the Merchant Adventures in Hope; and the Scholar Studies in Hope; and the Soldier Fights in Hope; and so for all Human Actions." (Sir Matthew Hale, "The vanity and vexation that ariseth from wordly hope and expectation," in *Contemplations Moral and Divine: in two parts*, 1675, p. 361)

Has the notion of hope changed over time, and with it the feelings we attribute to it? In order to experience hope, one must have a sense of something that is desired. This desire seems to be based on the knowledge that another reality could happen, and that there is a possibility of it happening beyond the emotional value of feeling that it will happen; therefore, a certain amount of 'evidence' of other such occurrences happening fuels our sense of hope. We know how to (search for) do much more nowadays than, say, a hundred years ago. And yet it seems that our hopeful longings only increase with the amount of information we consume, resulting in something resembling a closed loop of despair. With all the information we have at our fingertips, we are still not able to predict every outcome of any given situation, and hence we search for hope in the wrong places. This does not mean that the hopes of a hundred years ago were in any way lesser than those of today, but I would argue that, in the past, hope was based much more on our intuition and emotions than on the rational knowledge of a desired achievable outcome. How many of us have actually been faced with such dire prospects that rationality has left us completely and only raw emotion and hope remained? For most situations in life there is a backup—someone else who can explain things to us through a social media channel, someone else's experience presented to us on the silver platter of a globalised network meeting all of our daily needs. We can only hope that the engine of our sailing ship will start, yet without that backup, we must rely on our ability to bring the ship safely back home, even without the hope of a reliable engine. The hope to arrive home without the existence of a backup plan seems fundamentally purer than hoping that the engine will start. Maybe hope has turned into yet another commodity, which we cherish with a feeling of nostalgia? It used to be there, so let us still try to experience it, as it may be replaced by something else tomorrow. Do we still need hope, the sceptic would ask? What value are we assigning to hope, if the amount of information we consume daily clouds not only our judgment but, more importantly, our ability to feel and experience the emotions driven and championed by hope?

It is only through the eyes and ears of people that hope seems to come alive. This is arguably a Western notion of hope, yet nonetheless it is an idea which resonates with most of us. Maybe there is a deeper meaning as to why the anchor is the symbol associated with hope?

✳

Whether there were more or less disasters during the age of sail, when compared with the modern age, is difficult to say. What we do know for sure is that as electronic or digital tools were not available, mariners had to rely on their experience and intuition. They had to trust their feelings based on the sounds of the waves, the smell of the air, the direction of the wind and the material from which the seabed was made, as well as the position of the stars, the sun and the moon. Only with the invention of the chronograph were sailors able to determine their position more accurately. Having said this, sailors from Polynesia and Mesopotamia more than 10,000 years ago navigated the oceans by the stars alone, and there is evidence that they used the stars as mirror images of the outlines of shores they sailed to, linking individual stars in their minds to draw a map in the sky of what was below.

It is this particular relationship with nature that makes being out at sea such a rewarding experience. Anybody who says they are not scared when going out into the harsh conditions of the ocean is either a liar or a fool, Sir Robin Knox-Johnston, the well-known British sailor, once famously said in an interview.

But with all the experience and knowledge, there are always moments of misjudgement, danger or lack of foresight. The different coasts around the world have always been a challenge to seafarers. Navigating shallow sands or rocky shores with prevailing strong winds, which frequently rise to gale force, are only some of the dangers a ship and her crew can face.

Subjected to nature's forces when we are out at sea, we can neither create nor make the winds and tides work in our favour. We can merely harness her powers and learn each day how to safely navigate those places that are so alien to our human landlocked existence.

There are multiple accounts of wrecked ships and vanished crews, or saved passengers and happy endings. It is this juxtaposition of safety and risk that may be one of the attractions in wanting to go to sea.

A wrecked ship on the rocks off the east coast of England was described by a bystander during a storm in the 1800s; a gale was raging and a number of vessels were flying signals of distress in their rigging, and pilots and beachmen were out giving all assistance possible. In his book, Jack Mitchley describes "the new lifeboat, which was a thirty foot long, with a beam of ten feet six inches, double-ended wooden pulling boat, which was steered by a rudder at either end and was rowing ten oars" (Mitchley, *The Story of Lowestoft Lifeboats*,

Part 1: 1801–76, 1973). Even though this design was met with scepticism when it first appeared, it later proved to be one of the go-to plans for lifeboat construction around Britain and Europe.

Reservations around the design of the boat were mostly geographical in nature, as such a boat could be difficult to launch from a beach, pushing through the surf, without taking in large amounts of water even before out at sea. This led to adjustments in the vessel, depending on the type of beach, the launch facilities or the number of volunteers available to launch the boat.

In Mitchley's account, the launch to rescue went ahead despite gale-force winds and heavy swells. By the time the lifeboat reached the coal-laden Queen of the Tyne, she was on her beam ends and waves were breaking right over her. Her crew of eight had climbed the rigging, fearfully watching as the lifeboat approached, wondering how it could possibly reach them in time. As the brig rose and fell in the heavy swell, her yards were dipping into the water making a straightforward approach impossible. Despite the danger, the crew was saved from the topgallant yard, which at times even threatened to run the lifeboat through.

> "The Sailing ship was, of course, particularly prone to disaster when wind and sea rose in tumult. Driven Helplessly before the gale, and with few harbours of refuge where safety might be found—and these few often guarded by entrances more dangerous than the open coast itself—she would eventually crash on the rocks, the masts going overboard, her hull being pounded to pieces by the relentless seas, and her crews flung to their death in the surf."
> — CYRIL NOALL and GRAHAME FARR, *Wreck and Rescue Round the Cornish Coast*

Back in the day, such disasters could turn out to be gold mines for the local population, who would plunder the wrecked ship's cargo, or at least what was left of it—salvage wood, brass, copper or other valuables—and sometimes even rob and murder the crew for their possessions. Yet there were always the men and women, driven by empathy and pity, who rushed to their rescue, looking not for a quick enrichment of their own position, but to save lives. The barbarity of those who plundered and murdered, the motive often ascribed to poverty—the wrecker's excuse—fuelled the heroic self-sacrifice of life-saving crews and passengers of other passing ships. Unorganised at first, with only a handful of volunteers, these groups slowly grew to become the rescue services we have learned to appreciate and rely on around the world today.

The account of the *Viking* rescue, off the coast of Cornwall, describes the courage of the organised efforts to save human and ship.

"On April 2nd, 1872, there was a strong NNW gale and a tremendous sea breaking heavily along the whole north Cornish coast. The barque Viking, of Sunderland, with cargo of coals from Cardiff for the Mediterranean, had been desperately trying to keep away from the land, but had lost the unequal struggle. She found herself embayed, utterly unable to round Trevose Head, and in a desperate attempt to save lives, if not the ship, her master headed her towards the sandy beach of Harlyn into which a fearful surf was driving. Even so, there was a slightly better chance of the ship staying intact there long enough to save the crew. The news reached the town and the lifeboatmen hurried to the Cove to put into practise the scheme they had often tried at quarterly exercises. They launched the [life] boat and brought her back to Padstow. Meanwhile, ten horses had been obtained and brought the carriage from its house in the town to the outer slip. The boat was drawn on to its carriage and the team started along the quay. With several local officials to keep the way clear they took the hill at gallop, and when the tempo flagged many willing hands pushed and pulled wherever they could get a hand-hold. Once out of Padstow the pace quickened again and they were soon at Harlyn Bay, where the barque was now ashore but some distance off. Three men had taken the desperate step of trying to swim ashore and had been saved by brave spectators dashing into the surf. The sands were soft, the water shallow, and the gale right on shore, bringing very heavy breakers. By superhuman efforts the [life]boat was got afloat. She was filled by the first breaker, and as they strained at the oars against the sea and the gale their progress was so slow there were many who thought they would be beaten back. But [the lifeboat crew] slowly crept forward and reached the wreck at last. As she was lying bows-on there was virtually no shelter to be gained and the bat had to be kept under the bowsprit by means of a single line and constant use of the oars. Seas were repeatedly sweeping the length of the barque and over the foc'sle head into the lifeboat. The [barque's] mate first came down the line with a bundle in his coat which proved to be the master's baby. The baby was snatched by the [lifeboat's] bowman ad handed back into the boat, but the [barque's] mate missed his hold and was swept away to drown. At the same moment the rope parted and a succession of the seas sent the lifeboat back to the shore. The opportunity was taken to land the baby and again they battled their way back to the wreck. They then took off the master, his wife and boy, and three others. The cook refused the lifeboat, but lashed himself to ladder and jumped overboard. He was washed ashore insensible but revived after artificial respiration." (Noall and Farr, *Wreck and Rescue Round the Cornish Coast*).

This account very accurately describes the hardship, and the unbelievable willpower that lifeboat crews have, and had, to battle winds, tides and seas with oars alone. Hope comes in different forms and shapes, and while one hopes to be rescued, the rescuers hope they make it to the wreck, save her souls, and return home with all souls alive. Such an act, bringing life and death so close together, seems to awaken hidden and latent powers within most of us, overcoming tiredness, helplessness and weakness of body and mind.

Fishermen, pilots, deckhands, captains and mates, but also farmers, clerks, teachers, clergymen, doctors and nurses, have throughout the centuries risked their lives for others. Many have not returned in their attempt to save lives at sea.

When travelling up and down the coasts of Britain, the Netherlands or other countries bordered by the sea, there are a myriad of stories and memorials commemorating the lost rescuers who have sacrificed their lives for others. These stories, however, are a mix of sadness and pride. The year 1861 experienced one such tragic moment in the history of saving lives at sea. On February 9th, a heavy storm was raging across the North Sea and hit Whitby in the north of England very hard in the early hours of the morning. Locals awoke to winds so strong that it was impossible to stand on the pier without being blown over. The sea was boiling and while the wind screamed its way towards the town, desperate crews tried to enter the safety of the harbour. More than 200 ships were wrecked attempting to enter Whitby harbour, or outside the harbour in open water trying to survive the tempest. Of the ships that managed to enter the harbour, another thirty were so badly damaged they sank in port.

"By 8.30am, the lifeboat crew had launched their first rescue, successfully saving the crew of the *John and Ann*.

"Not long after they returned, they were called out again to assist a schooner, Gamma, who had run aground. After their second successful rescue, the crew celebrated with a glass of grog at the station. At 11.30am, the Clara was seen heading for shore, close to the wreck of the Gamma. The lifeboat crew rowed out to rescue the crew, and the ship broke up shortly after they left the scene. The crew each had another drink back at the station, feeling tired and hungry from their exhausting morning. Two more vessels were spotted coming ashore, Utility and Roe. Once more, the lifeboat crew rowed out to save both crews. Spectators began to gather onshore to cheer the lifeboat crew. They returned at midday and took their third glass of grog. By 2pm, the violent gales were still at full force. Harbourmaster Mr Tose and Coxswain John Storr decided that if more vessels came in, they would not respond—the lifeboat would be of little use at a high tide. Shortly afterwards, the Flora and the Merchant were spotted in trouble. The Flora successfully glided into the harbour, but the Merchant ran ashore.

"Although they'd agreed not to respond, the Whitby lifeboat crew couldn't stand by and watch the Merchant sink. As they manoeuvred towards the stricken collier, a powerful wave caught the stern of the lifeboat, capsizing it and throwing the crew overboard.

"A huge crowd watched helplessly from shore as the crew struggled in the fierce sea. Sadly, all but one of the crew drowned. The sole survivor was Henry Freeman, who was on his first call out. His life was saved by the new design of cork lifejacket he wore, donated by the RNLI." (https://rnli.org/about-us/our-history/timeline/1861-whitby-lifeboat-disaster, retrieved 31/10/2023).

Since 1810, more than 600 volunteers in Great Britain have lost their lives at sea: eight men drowned when their lifeboat, departing from Hoylake lifeboat station, capsized in heavy seas to rescue a trawler in 1810; five men died when huge waves fell on the Great Yarmouth lifeboat, drowning both boat and crew in 1824; three members of the Liverpool lifeboat crew and nine passengers drowned when their boat capsized; John James, crew member of the Aberystwyth lifeboat station, died of exhaustion after a long shift in 1877; in 1939, the St Ives lifeboat capsized three times and righted itself three times, each time losing one of her crew of eight: only one person survived; and the list continues.

Whether we go to sea as merchant mariners, fishermen, lifeboat crew or naval marines, or because we are seeking to push the boundaries of our own comfort zone, it is hope that accompanies us on this endeavour—hope that we will make it safely back home, hope that we will find what we were looking for, hope that we will rescue the ones in desperate need, or hope that we ourselves will be rescued, with our hopes still alive.

A Dose of Realism!

Greg Powlesland

Sailing the 1885, 27-foot gaff-rigged yacht *Collinette*, engineless and single-handed, to Douarnenez from Helford, Cornwall, and back.

12th August 1998. Set main and foresail and leave mooring at 2pm. Wind north-northeast 3 to 4 Beaufort scale. Last of the ebb taking us down river two miles with the tide. Tack out past the headlands and sail close hauled heading for the Manacles buoy. Stream the patent log, once round, ease sheets for a pleasant run towards the Lizard. 5pm. Ten nautical miles sailed. Goonhilly Earth Station in the distance. Wind backs to north by west. Making 5 knots over the ground and by 6.30pm the Lizard headland is just visible dropping away astern. Wind now a steady force 4, a gorgeous sunset and *Collinette* dipping to the rising waves, occasionally splashing her long boom end into the sea crests as we swoop forward. Light the oil nav lights and cabin lamp. 31 nautical miles travelled by 9pm. Chart position 49°34′ N −04°58′ long. As well as sailing with trailing log and charts, I had acquired a mobile G P S, at the time a relatively new invention. With this I was able to check my chart positions occasionally. At 11.15pm the crescent moon rises in her reclining chair while dressed in woollen robes. A vast tanker passes astern as we enter the northern shipping lanes and turns his search light onto our sails before the black spectre throbs its way into the night gloom. It's a judgment lottery choosing a course through the lanes, which is best achieved at right angles, but the speed of some of these leviathans can be deceptive, sometimes requiring a rapid tack to get out of the way. It's a warm night and a shooting star darts unexpectedly across the heavens. Midnight, 47 nautical miles travelled and I catch a glimpse of the flash of light from the Isle of Vierge. Brittany ahead! We are halfway across the channel. I play a few tunes on the concertina whilst nudging the tiller periodically with an elbow, warding off the desire to sleep. From the cockpit, miniature teak doors open outward from the snug interior where a wood burning cooking range is handy to port and nav table to starboard. Thus hot soup at night is a great occasion and chart positions can be marked. By 4am the wind has dropped to a force 2 to 3. Our average speed has been 4.5 knots. Suddenly a fish lands on the counter, perhaps drawn by the stern oil lamp. Log 65 nautical miles. In the velvet black dark of night the great canopy of stars wheeling overhead is an ethereal experience from a small lone boat far from land and in almost dead silence, apart from the gentle shushing of the bow wave. A damp cool of early morning dew accompanies a subtle dawn light creeping up from the northeast horizon. A grand crimson, yellow-streaked dawn awakening above a steel grey sea and the wind dies to a whisper. The shore lights of northern Brittany dwindle in a mist and by 9am we are about ten miles from the French coast. The tide and a whisper of following wind give 3 knots over the ground towards the Chenal du Four. The sun is getting hot, rising from a clear blue haze. Cat's paws of negligible wind die away by midday and by 3.15pm the towed log, now reading 84 miles, hangs vertical in a sullen reflective sea. No wind and the changed tide now floating *Collinette* back from whence we came. The cotton sails flap and scuffle as we aimlessly wallow on a greasy puddled sea, the harsh sun reflecting an oblivion of nothing but water and sky. Our position is well north of the Isle d'Ouessant and by 8pm the possibility of another night without sleep with no wind and no progress. Our drift with the turn of the tide is towards the shipping lanes, with a bank of fog looming on the horizon. A deep throbbing sound from oil tankers beyond sight creates a tense and sombre mood to this trance-like situation. A French warship threateningly circles our position but leaves, perhaps guessing that the Douarnenez festival is our destination. With no wind I can ill afford to drift right into the shipping lanes. Towards evening I spy a little motor fishing boat about a mile away. The possibility of a tow? I light a flare to garner his attention but to no avail as I am between him and the setting sun. As darkness envelopes our watery world, I put out a call on the radio to see if anyone is heading towards the coast only three miles away. Amazingly, a boat called *Windsong* answered my call and offered a tow into the Chenal du Four, where I could anchor as it was calm. They arrived before the hour was up, a very friendly sailor with his family on their way to Ireland, but happy to tow us north to the coast at Pointe du Corsen in the Chenal du Four. They swung me off the beach by 1.30am where I cast off the tow with a shout of thanks to David Bearn and farewell. I was then able to use the sculling oar to edge into a safe depth of 24 feet at low tide to anchor off, with a heavy ground swell breaking in a roar on the pure sands 300 meters beyond. Here I was finally able to sleep after being continuously on watch for over two days.

14th August, 6.30am. Wake up to a bright morning and a light northeast breeze. Set main, fore and topsails, thirty miles to go and a good tide up the Chenal du Four. The current here can exceed 5 knots, so we must make the most of it before the change at 1.30pm. We shoot past La Parquette buoy, out from Camaret, then sail round the Cap de la Chèvre with wind abeam giving a straight run at 6 knots to anchor off Douarnenez by evening. The festival is in full swing with sea shanties and song, wine and fellowship in abundance. Over the next four days I take the opportunity to catch up on sleep, overhaul the rig, and enjoy 'moules et frites' and 'le baguette'! *Kaskelot*, the square rigger from Charlestown in Cornwall, is alongside the quay, where I am able to shower curtesy of Captain John Bates, before preparing for the return voyage.

Tuesday 18th August, 10.30am. Cast off under full sail from rafted up vessels in very light wind, getting a good northeaster out in the bay which dies off by 1pm, followed by a wind change to west by north. 2pm. The lifting wire for the centreboard chafes through but fortunately I had fitted a preventer which now takes the weight of the board, but for some reason it will not lift on the winch? So we must not venture into the shallows. *Collinette* only draws 3 feet 6 inches with the board up, but 6 feet with it down. 2.30pm. Pass Le Boue. The rock is not buoyed and great waves crash around it. See a strange creature splashing in the waves but cannot figure out what it is? Wind now 3 to 4. We are tacking north. And by 7.30pm pass Le Parquette buoy and the tide helps in sailing up the Chenal du Four where I head for some presumed shore-side lights; however, they turn out to be fishing boats. I sail past them finding a wide sandy bay where I glide in close and then tack out to anchor in 4 fathoms. Set oil riding light and dive below for supper of cheese and wine. A big swell swills *Collinette* around, bouncing and rolling with the steel centreboard banging all night as a result of not being able to raise it, so hardly any sleep. Miss the shipping forecast and note fog at 6am. However, a beautiful morning gives me the time to repair the centreboard lifting rope. Stow the pram dingy upside down on the coach roof, have breakfast, raise sail and weigh anchor, which is raised by hand.

Wednesday 19th August, 10.30am. Leave glorious sandy beach astern. Wind north force 3. Dave Luck's galion appears out of Le Conquet and friends who I met in Douarnenez are sailing within hailing distance. They are heading home but more west to allow for possible wind change. Tide setting us out nicely, position N 48.30.8–W 4.54.4. Course 305. Making 2 knots over the ground. 3.30pm. Tack to the north. Making northeast 1/4N. Very light airs. Midnight. Cold now and through the first shipping lanes. Log 21 miles. Beans on toast! 1.30am. Completely becalmed. A remarkably clear starry night. The Milky Way is a wreath of silk tendrils aloft and the sea sparkles with magical phosphorescence. Forecast, Plymouth, west 3 to 4 then southwest 25 knots even force 7. This is a lot of wind for little *Collinette* I note with a hint of anxiety. At 4.30am the wind pipes up 4 to 5 with rain. I jump to lower the working topsail and jib the sail. One normally might remove these sails at night, but wanting to gain miles homeward I retained them until the increase in wind. The sea was still relatively quiet and by pointing up into the wind and setting the tiller, the boat rode quietly as I went forward, hauled down and stowed the sails while hooked on by a rope harness. Check the oil lamps. Burning brightly! Log 42 miles and soon to cross the next shipping lanes. No close encounters this time and now sailing at a fast 5 knots. A grey dawn with whitecaps and by 8.30am wind up to a steady force 5 with more to come. I decide to heave to in the billowing seas and spend the next hour getting in a full three reefs and making sure everything about the deck and 12-foot bowsprit is all secure. Being single-handed everything takes a lot of time, heaving down with block and tackle and putting on extra lashings, etc. I retain the full foresail as the boat is thus better balanced, but it's not a reassuring outlook with the prospect of a gale building. Ease out sails and now reaching at 5.2 knots due north. Tide ebbing until midday, position N 49.11.04–W 04.37.83.

Thursday 20th August. 58 miles north of Chenal du Four. By midday the sea had eased a bit but with the change of the tide and an increase in wind to force 6, the sea became more vicious by 3pm. A big sea was now running, splashing the odd bucketful into the cockpit. 75 miles travelled now with the southwest wind continuing to increase. *Collinette* is handling well but the reefed main is still too much sail. Hoping to reach the lee of the Lizard before nightfall. In the cabin the bilge is swilling with sea water which I am able to mostly pump out by hand from the cockpit. Everything is now wet in the cabin below, as I hastily eat a sandwich lunch, washed down with sea spray as we are being thrown around. I calculate that land should be sited by 6.30pm as our average speed has risen to 6 or 7 knots. Remarkable for a vessel of 22-foot waterline, but because she is shallow she skates at speed down the waves. Great Atlantic waves now with frothing tops wall up in advancing rows heading up channel as we glide nimbly onward, sometimes in a cloud of wind-blown spray. The wind steadily increases producing spindrift white streaks all around. Flying skud, crest and trough, we are well heeled over with wave crests occasionally breaking over the counter and bow and lolloping over the dingy lashed down over the cabin. No land but a trawler sited at 6.30pm. I eat early supper of beans and cheese on bread whilst huddled in the cabin hatchway beneath a makeshift canvas awning, the cabin doors closed to avoid flooding by flying sea, as *Collinette*'s freeboard is only 18 inches aft. There is a great roaring all around and a constant humming from bar taut hemp rope and wire rig. The solid pitch pine bowsprit takes regular duckings and bends to the strain of the salt-soaked cotton foresail. I gradually ease sheets to spill wind in the now gale-force wind and at 7.30pm site the Cornish coast in a shroud gloom of grey and mist. 20 miles off Fowey; maybe we could enter there by dusk. Impossible to light the nav lights without heaving to so I decide to crack on. There has been a slight let up in the wind and sea, perhaps the distant lee of the Lizard, but as night falls it builds again and backs south of west. Now it's more of a run and it's all I can do to steer with the tiller, requiring its handling from full starboard to port in order to keep us on course and avoid broaching. With every heavy roll the end of the boom dives into the cresting sea and then lifts out shaking off cascades of the salty brine. I possibly could have scandalised the reefed mainsail but not easy to accomplish single-handed in these conditions and we were soon to get under the lee of the distant Dodman Point. Darkness has now descended and a full gale is blowing. We scream down monster waves, short and sharp as the tide is now against us. It feels like a 12 knot sleigh ride, the counter is constantly awash and white water everywhere. I see the black looming Dodman in the dusk, then the lights of Par, then Fowey. Even with the tiller fully over the boat yaws off across the marching cresting waves. Water streams continuously along the decks beside the cockpit coaming, but never overwhelms it. A spectacular run. No one in sight! How many epic voyage adventures over the ages have been lost in history, unreported? Though fearsome this is also an exciting experience. Again, I have had no proper sleep for two nights and become unsure of the entrance to Fowey in a now pitch black night, so I decide to heave to off Par bay in order to light the oil lamps and shorten sail. *Collinette* pitches in the unseen seas with the gale howling in the rig. I crawl into the dark, soaking cabin to retrieve the lamps, the matches are soaked but somehow I manage a spark to light the paraffin wicks. Attempting any task in extreme weather single-handed takes a lot of time. One trips over life lines then gets tangled in the harness clip rope while crawling around the tiny deck. One also has to hang on with one arm as the boat arcs wildly and leaps around in the tossing waves. On finally getting the three lamps lit and in position I discovered that the main sheet had caught on the stern light bracket and bent it sideways extinguishing the flame. Then the jib sheet knocked out the flame of the starboard light. Relighted I bore off with the mainsail scandalised. I reckoned it was about force 7 at this point but *Collinette* was handling it well with rain and spray seeping down my neck and filling my shoes. Oh the joys of adventure! Soon I spy the port entrance and as we approach the seas are finally mellowed and we glide by Readymoney Cove into the safety of Fowey Harbour. Feeling very tired but relieved to be in calm water, I sail around the estuary harbour enclosed by steep-sided slopes of ancient oaks and the huddled dwellings of Fowey town, with welcoming twinkling lights beckoning through veils of streaming rain, but no free mooring could be found. Thus I was relieved when Tony from sv *Tangaroa* appeared in his rubber dingy and helped me moor up alongside the harbour pontoon. Completely soaked and 'spaced out' I squelch up to the Luck's house in town, where I had hoped to attend their evening party, but it's midnight and they finished at 10pm! On opening the front door they were shocked at my appearance, thinking I was a vagrant. I was unrecognisable as I had lamp black streaked with salt and rain water all over my face. After a grand mug of tea I headed back to sleep in the cold wet cabin on *Collinette*, not waking until 9.30am. Go ashore for a few stores and a hearty English breakfast before casting off to go alongside Dave Luck's galion, *Mon Rêve*, in Pill Creek. Dave had motor sailed back from Douarnenez avoiding the gale. It was 6pm before I started to clear up down below on *Col-linette*, lighting the wood stove to dry everything out. By 9.30pm all was snug again and we headed ashore to listen to the town's silver band playing on the town quay.

22nd August. Fowey to Helford. Up at 9am. Foggy. Set full main and topsail. Little wind. I get a tow out from Dave, cast off, set foresail and slowly tack out amongst the racing Troy boats. Rain then a flat calm. Breakfast at 12pm. Shipping forecast giving west-southwest 4 to 6. Suddenly up springs a strong wind from the north heeling the boat and tipping the marmalade pot upside down onto the cabin sole. Fog clears near the Dodman at 1.30pm and by 3.30 we are south of St Anthony Lighthouse. 5pm at the entrance to the Helford we sail up to a motorboat with a fishing line round his propellor. Take him in tow! Up to Helford with the gusty north wind giving us a beam reach. A Whitbread yacht sails in astern having left Fowey at the same time as us. Finally at 6.30pm gently sail up to Tremerlin quay and make fast under the lee of the overhanging twisted old oak trees, our single-handed engineless voyage complete.

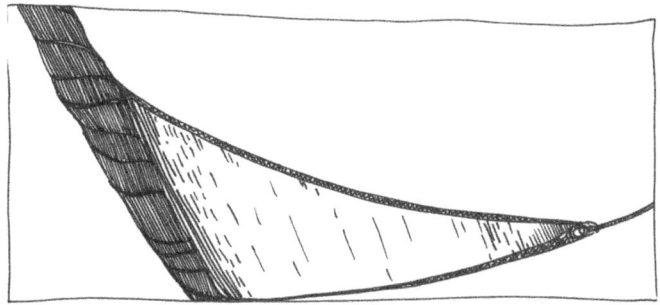

Listening to Wild

Rose May Ravetz

"Don't waste your wildness: it is precious and necessary."
— JAY GRIFFITHS

When I was nineteen, I left Manchester with a rucksack, a tent and a folder holding various poems and song lyrics related to the sea. Only four months previously I had decided to sail across the Atlantic, having never before been on a sailing boat.

"I'm leavin' my family
And leavin' my friends
My body's at home
But my heart's in the wind
Where the clouds are like headlines
On a new front page sky

My tears are salt water
And the moon's full and high"

— TOM WAITS

One of the songs I had learned, and written the lyrics down for, was "Shiver Me Timbers" by Tom Waits. Waits' words gave expression to the nostalgia, romance and stubbornness that I was feeling as I left my home and family, and stepped out into this unknown adventure. More than anything, I wanted to travel like the adventurers of old—before package holidays and English-speaking youth hostels existed. Travelling with few belongings, no connection to home, and an open heart in place of a plan, I wanted, with unwavering certainty, to be wild.

Wild. This word had whispered its companionship and urgency to me since I was fifteen, when I was given a book by the same name. Written by Jay Griffiths in 2006, *Wild: An Elemental Journey* is a book so unique I find it difficult to describe in one sentence. It embodies its title, being both anarchic and magnificent. Always in my rucksack, my copy was battered and held together by tape. Its impression on me was profound.

Setting out as a late teen, the word 'Wild' gave me the strength to seek the unknown. Alongside wanting to be a swashbuckling discoverer, I also wanted to immerse myself in the wilderness of our planet. I wanted to become submerged in the elements; boundaries blurred so that I didn't know what was me and what was ocean, rain, forest or mud.

Crossing an ocean on a small boat. The idea seemed the epitome of adventure and wildness, all at once. I was completely unaware of what it really meant to cross an ocean, and I put unreserved trust in the hands of the crew who would invite me to join them. From the Canaries to the Caribbean, we followed the trade winds and swept across the globe. As a 'green hand' on this passage, it was messy and challenging, whilst equally utterly awe-inspiring. I spent long, rolling hours sitting on the bow, atop the safety pulpit railing, the closest I could be to the vast, undulating ocean. Nights were lit by glimmering skies and seas, the horizon lost in stars and phosphorescence—our planet and our universe no longer divided. A far cry from Manchester's paved streets and high-rise buildings, I vowed to continue on the journey.

In the years that followed, I travelled long distances under sail. I began to understand how sailing worked and to discern what made for a good sailor. My experience broadened and life at sea became part of me.

I read old books about seafaring and realised the depth of our maritime history. I started questioning how I had learned to sail: on a modern yacht fitted with GPS, autopilot and an engine. I saw that there was much, much more to learn, more than I had ever imagined as a dreamy teenager in Manchester. How was it that huge ships of times past could manoeuvre under sail alone when a small yacht today would not contemplate leaving harbour without an engine?

The search for adventure and the wild was not complete. Although I had found sailing, there was still a disconnect between the boat, the elements, and the humans. We acted as if the oceans, the wind and the fish, were ours for the taking, mere objects that we could make use of when available. Coming into port, fire up the engine and take down the sails. Stop feeling the wind, for the conversation is over.

To sail is to partake in the dance of life. A grand statement, perhaps, but when the sails lift and the boat gains momentum, the sailor knows this to be true. Releasing the mooring line, pulling the halyard, trimming the sheets; by setting sail, we humans see the tangible interaction between ourselves and nature. We enter into a dialogue with that which surrounds us. We can shape the dialogue, perhaps, but we cannot control it. If we are lucky, we will be equal to these elemental forces. As much as we talk, in this conversation, we are obliged to listen.

We have, as a society, fallen under the illusion that we are somehow separate from nature. We believe that our intelligence surpasses that of the natural worlds. As individuals we might visit nature, we may enjoy her presence, but our belief that we are separate keeps us distant. The life systems that sustain us happen far away, over there, not in and around us. We do not know ourselves to be wild.

The auxiliary engine is an invention that has brought unprecedented change, both for better and for worse. An astounding development, when used from the perspective of separation, has proved to be dangerous. Though undeniable good fortune has resulted from the invention, we are also witnessing a breakdown of our natural world caused, in part, by our engines. It is not the machine itself that is problematic but the deeply seated belief in our separateness that has informed how we have used it.

Sailing on board a vessel fitted with an auxiliary engine is incredibly convenient. We can go further, worry less, fit into tight spaces, and travel against wind and tide—to name just a few of the many benefits. In essence, we overcome nature. We dominate the dialogue, talking over the elements and imposing our will. We believe this is pragmatic—we wish to have a certain experience, and we believe it is acceptable to force our way through to reach this experience. We think we are entitled to enjoy ourselves, and because we believe we are separate from nature, it feels permissible to take what we want from her.

The truth is we are nature. Made up of chemical elements formed in stars, we share the same materials as everything around us. We grow with nourishment from the food growing in our soil, the sun's energy, and the clouds condensing their water. Though our modern society has persuaded us otherwise, there is no separation between us and the natural world—none, other than the ideas in our head. We could not survive without the biodiversity and the climate that blesses our planet. In turn, nature may benefit from us, too. Our capacity for reflection is a gift if we use it wisely: if we could stop talking, and listen.

To sail engineless is to learn how to listen. Without the possibility of domination, the engineless mariner relies upon their skill and their ability to tune in. Feel the brush of wind upon the cheek not just once, but constantly, quietly tracking its variance. The gentle sweep of the current, always lessening, growing or slack, different in every corner, every turn of the shore. The hull, its depth in the water, how clean or barnacled it is, and the distribution of weight—details are important. Power lies in the subtle. To sail like this is to orchestrate within the scope of the earth's offerings. To sail like this is to belong to our planet.

There are limitations to sailing engineless. It may mean that a particular place is not as easy to get to, that our choice is restrained. If we are short on time, we may have to reduce our distance to suit. Our arrival time is never guaranteed, our overall plan always subject to change. It is a difficult fact that marine services are not particularly accommodating of engineless craft, and reverse parking into a finger berth is somewhat impossible under sail. Sailors are nothing if not resourceful, however, and these boundaries can be extended; traditional skills such as kedging, warping and rowing all add to our vocabulary. There are, however, still limits.

Though we are under the impression that we deserve to have what we want, perhaps we need to question our aversion to limits. What matters more: the details of what we experience, or how we experience the details?

Manoeuvring under sail alone offers us a chance to engage our power of agency, whilst encountering and responding to the will of forces around us. It is this dance that reminds us of the greater whole of which we are a part. Provided the necessary steps are taken to ensure safety, there is nothing more enlivening, empowering and connection-forming than experiencing this dance. Whether it takes place 500 yards from the mooring or further afield doesn't matter—it does not have to be a long trip to be a memorable voyage.

Whether we have an engine or not, whether we sail or not, humanity would benefit if we could listen better. If we could slow down enough to feel the gentle air whispering, notice the leaves shimmering, that worm wriggling, nurturing the soil that holds our next meal. See the tide gently stalling and beginning to flow the other way. So many tiny moments make up our experience on this earth; if we can only hear the call, we might be able to respond, to partake in this elemental conversation. If we did, we might find no reason to get somewhere particular. We may discover that we are already home, and that our home is gorgeous.

One poem

Catharina Vergeer

dreaming in the dew point
under the cover of rain
rocking through the rendition
of geometries in the water
where the keepers of radical solitude
seek a shelter of silence

*

dromen in het dauwpunt
onder de dekking van regen
wiegend door de vertolking
van geometrieën in het water
waar de bewaarders van radicale eenzaamheid
zoeken naar een schuilplaats van stilte

Glossary

BOW   The front of a boat.

BOWSPRIT   A large spar projecting forwards from the ship's bow.

BOW WAVE   The wave that forms at the bow of a ship when it moves through the water.

BREAKWATER   An offshore structure (such as a wall) to protect a harbour or beach from the force of the waves.

BUNT   The middle section of a sail.

CANT, *to*   Turning a ship's head one way or another, according to requirement, when weighing anchor or moving from a mooring.

CARABINER   A D-shaped or oblong metal ring with one spring-hinged side that is used especially in climbing for attaching two things, for example, a harness and a rope.

CATAMARAN   A yacht or boat with two hulls parallel to each other that is much more stable than a monohull boat. They are mainly used for recreational purposes.

CLEW   The bottom back corner of the sail (furthest from the mast).

CLOSE HAULED   This is sailing as close to the wind as you can go.

COAMING   This is any vertical surface on a ship designed to deflect or prevent entry of water.

CRABBER   An English brand of sailboats, the Cornish Crabber was designed by naval architect Roger Dongray in the early 1970s in Rock, a fishing village in North Cornwall. The first Cornish Crabber was made of plywood in 1973.

DISMAST, *to*   To break or force down the mast or masts of a ship, for example, during a storm.

DOWNHAUL   A line which is part of the rigging on a sailboat; it applies downward force on a spar or sail.

DREDGER   This is a boat that tows weighted nets along the bottom of the sea in order to catch oysters or mussels.

HALYARD   A halyard or halliard is a line (rope) that is used to hoist a ladder, sail, flag or yard.

HELM   The part of a boat or ship that is used to steer it using a tiller, wheel, rudder, etc.

"IRON TOPSAIL"   Diesel engine on a boat.

KEDGING   Kedging is using anchors to manoeuvre or move a vessel.

KEELER   A type of sailboat that is designed for stability and long-distance cruising. They are typically larger and heavier than other sailboats, with a deep keel that provides stability in rough waters.

KETCH   A two-masted, fore-and-aft rigged sailing boat with a mizzenmast stepped forward of the rudder and smaller than its foremast.

LONG LINER   A fishing vessel that uses a long main line supported by floats, with shorter lines attached to it with baited hooks at their lower point. Shooting of the long line is done over the stern. The lines are hauled, the catch removed, the hooks rebaited, and the line reshot.

LUGGER   A small fishing boat that has one or more lug sails on its masts.

MACKEREL DRIFTER   A type of fishing vessel (sailing or steam), the sails of which or its supporting sail (in a steam boat) are positioned in such a way so that it 'drifts' over the shoal of fish, allowing the lines to catch the mackerel. It often has a rather flat-bottomed hull.

MIRROR   A type of popular sailing dinghy, named after the Daily Mirror, a UK newspaper with a largely working-class distribution. The Mirror was, from the start, promoted as an affordable boat, and it has done a great deal to make dinghy sailing accessible.

MIZZEN   The mast behind the ship's main mast.

PILOT CUTTER   A Bristol Channel pilot cutter is a type of sailing boat used until the early part of the 20th century to deliver and collect pilots to and from merchant vessels using ports in the Bristol Channel.

REEF, *to*   Reefing is to reduce the size of a sail—it not only helps keep the boat more upright but reduces a lot of dangerous strain on the boat and rig, and can make her easier to steer.

RUDDER   A flat piece, hinged vertically, near the stern of a ship or boat for steering.

SCULL, *to*   Sculling is to use a single oar that rests in a notch in the stern of a boat; the blade is swept from side to side in the water, with a twist at the end of each stroke to angle it to provide thrust. Sculling is also a term used to refer to rowing with two oars, as opposed to having one oar per rower, which is referred to as pulling.

SHEERLINE   The longitudinal curve of the rail or decks, which shows the variation in height above water or throughout a vessel's entire length.

SPINNAKER   A sail designed specifically for sailing off the wind on courses between a reach (wind at 90° to the course) to downwind (course in the same direction as the wind). Spinnakers are constructed of lightweight fabric, usually nylon, and are often brightly coloured.

STAYSAIL   An auxiliary sail, often triangular, set to catch the wind, as between the masts of a yawl (mizzen staysail), aft of a spinnaker (spinnaker staysail), etc.

STERN   The rear of a boat.

TACK, *to*   Tacking is a manoeuvre used to change the direction of a sailboat when sailing upwind or at an angle to the wind. It is a fundamental technique for changing the side of the boat that faces into the wind in order to make progress towards a desired destination.

TALL SHIP   A large traditionally, often square, rigged sailing ship with a tall mast or masts.

TENDER   A smaller boat that is used to take passengers to and from a larger vessel.

TOPGALLANT YARD   The yard from which a topgallant sail is set on a square-rigged sailing vessel, above the topsail or topsails.

TRAWLER   A commercial fishing vessel designed to operate fishing trawls. Trawling is a method of fishing that involves actively dragging or pulling a trawl through the water behind one or more trawlers.

TROG, *to*   To drift sideways.

TUMBLEHOME   A term describing a hull which grows narrower than its beam above the waterline.

WARPING   Warping is to move or manoeuvre a vessel using just ropes.

YARD   A large wooden or metal spar crossing the masts of a sailing vessel horizontally or diagonally, from which sails are set.

Acknowledgements

Our thanks go to the "fair winds and following seas", to Mother Nature, to the breeze that shakes the barley on the lands that feed us, to that same wind that blows our sails in the direction of our destiny. As long as humanity lives, we have this planet to thank, with all her secrets, all her pleasures and beauty. Let us protect her, with all the knowledge, skills and blessings we have.

Special thanks go to a few people who have guided us through words and images: Ken Turner, Amanda Ravetz, Gareth Evans, Penny Iremonger, Jacqui Knight, Martijn Dentant and Ashley Fields. The publisher would also like to thank Diederik Dijkstra, who took her sailing when she was twelve, and Arjan Evers, who brought her and Artur Jaschke sailing across the North Sea; it changed our lives.

About the Publisher

The New Menard Press is the British imprint of HetMoet Publishing, an indie press based on a historic sailing barge in Amsterdam, the Netherlands, founded by Elte Rauch in 2018. The Menard Press was founded by Anthony Rudolf in 1969.

Please get in touch at info@thenewmenardpress.com
Subscribe to our newsletter, visit: www.thenewmenardpress.com
Follow us on Instagram: @thenew_menardpress

Author Biographies

HUW WAHL is a filmmaker and artist who has earned international recognition, winning awards and showcasing his work globally. With funding from organisations like the Henry Moore Foundation, Arts Council England and the Royal Photographic Society, he explores the transformative potential of creative action through the material qualities of moving images, driven by his belief in film's power to open experiences and ideas for communal change.

WIEBE RADSTAKE is a skipper aboard *Vrijbuiter*. He grew up in Zeeland and has been sailing with the charter vessels through the Netherlands for over eighteen years. Eight years ago, he joined Fairtransport, responsible for shipping products entirely under sail throughout Europe and South and Central America. In addition to sailing, Wiebe is a musician and reads and writes as much as possible. He is married to Suzan and they live aboard a Dutch barge with their young children. Suzan also sails and joined the *Tres Hombres* amongst other vessels.

STEVIE HUNT grew up in Sheffield and first sailed when he was five. He voraciously devoured books on the subject—mostly traditional sail—and discovered the sailing barges of the East Coast. His work experience at fifteen was two weeks on a sailing barge, which opened the doors to a career on the water that took in barges, smacks and yachts in various formats of work—mostly chartering and youth sail training. He bought *Birubi* in 2013, and removed the engine during a substantial restoration.

RICHARD TITCHENER grew up in Brightlingsea and became fascinated by its waterside and, later, by the utility of sailing smacks. He found a hobby in sailing them, culminating many years later in rebuilding the *Sallie*. In 1994, Richard turned his hobby into a profession as a bargeman and in 2007, set up the Sea-Change Sailing Trust with his partner, Hilary, using hired vessels to develop its sail training while appealing for funds to build the *Blue Mermaid*. She was built in the UK and commissioned in 2019, and sails with around 200 people each year.

MIKE JACKSON is a lifelong recreational sailor, living in North Wales, who recently retired from his work as a researcher in mental health and as an NHS clinical psychologist. He specialised for many years in working with young people who have had psychotic disorders. In recent times, in partnership with the Cirdan Sailing Trust, Mike developed the 'Early intervention in psychosis Voyage to Recovery' projects, which have seen teams of young people from around the UK collectively circumnavigate the country in a 40-tonne wooden ketch.

JESSICA TAGGART ROSE is a writer and editor concerned with humanity, nature and how they interact. Her work has been published in the *Letters to the Earth*, Green Ink's *Wild Weather* anthologies, *Confluence Magazine* and a range of zines. Jessica is a founding member of Poets for the Planet and one half of the Promenade duo. She lives in Margate.

EMMA RAULT is a writer and a literary translator from Dutch and German. Her work has appeared in *Guernica*, the *LA Review of Books*, *Literary Hub* and elsewhere. Her most recent translation is *We Had to Remove This Post* by Hanna Bervoets, published by Harper (US) and Picador (UK). Originally from the Netherlands, she lives on unceded Gabrielino-Tongva land (and waters) in Los Angeles.

JUDE BRICKHILL is a writer and a sailor who has helmed innumerable sailing vessels for over fifty years: racing dinghies at university in South Africa, a range of small and large boats during her time as a maritime journalist, and *Guide Me*, the 1911 engineless Looe mackerel drifter, found and restored by her husband and herself in Cornwall.

ARTUR C. JASCHKE is a neuro-musicologist currently researching the effects of music-based therapies and interventions in neurodiverse children at the University of Cambridge. After his PhD he also completed the Enkhuizer Zeevaart School in the Netherlands and became first officer on sailing Tall ships. He lives on a historic sailing barge, likes to go on long walks with his Border Collie and is an active volunteer at the RNLI.

GREG POWLESLAND studied sculpture and fine arts at Colchester, St Martins and Chelsea art schools whose artwork has been exhibited at the Royal Academy London. He also worked as a design tutor at the John Makepeace school for craftsmen in wood. In 1974, Greg sailed as a rigger on a replica *Golden Hinde* and worked as shipwright aboard their museum ship *Balclutha*, including carving a replacement figurehead. He now manages the restoration of yachts, such as *Marigold*, *Collinette* and *Patna*.

ROSE MAY RAVETZ started sailing at nineteen, when she crossed the Atlantic Ocean. She spent four years on various ocean crossings, eventually reaching New Zealand, from where she sailed back to Europe as a professional crew member on the famous classic schooner, *Atlantic*. Since her return, she has worked for sail-cargo initiatives and sail-training charities, and as a traditional rigger on museum ships including the *Cutty Sark* and *HMS Gannet*. Rose is now studying for a BA in Philosophy and Sustainability.

CATHARINA VERGEER is a visual artist and filmmaker based in Amsterdam. She studied Image and Language at the Gerrit Rietveld Academy and is currently pursuing her MA at The Netherlands Film Academy. Her ongoing practice draws from the relations that coalesce between the societal fabrics of gestures and their meanings. This culminated in a study that magnifies language barriers and underlines the stratification of language. She uses a broad conception of language that is not limited to writing or speech.

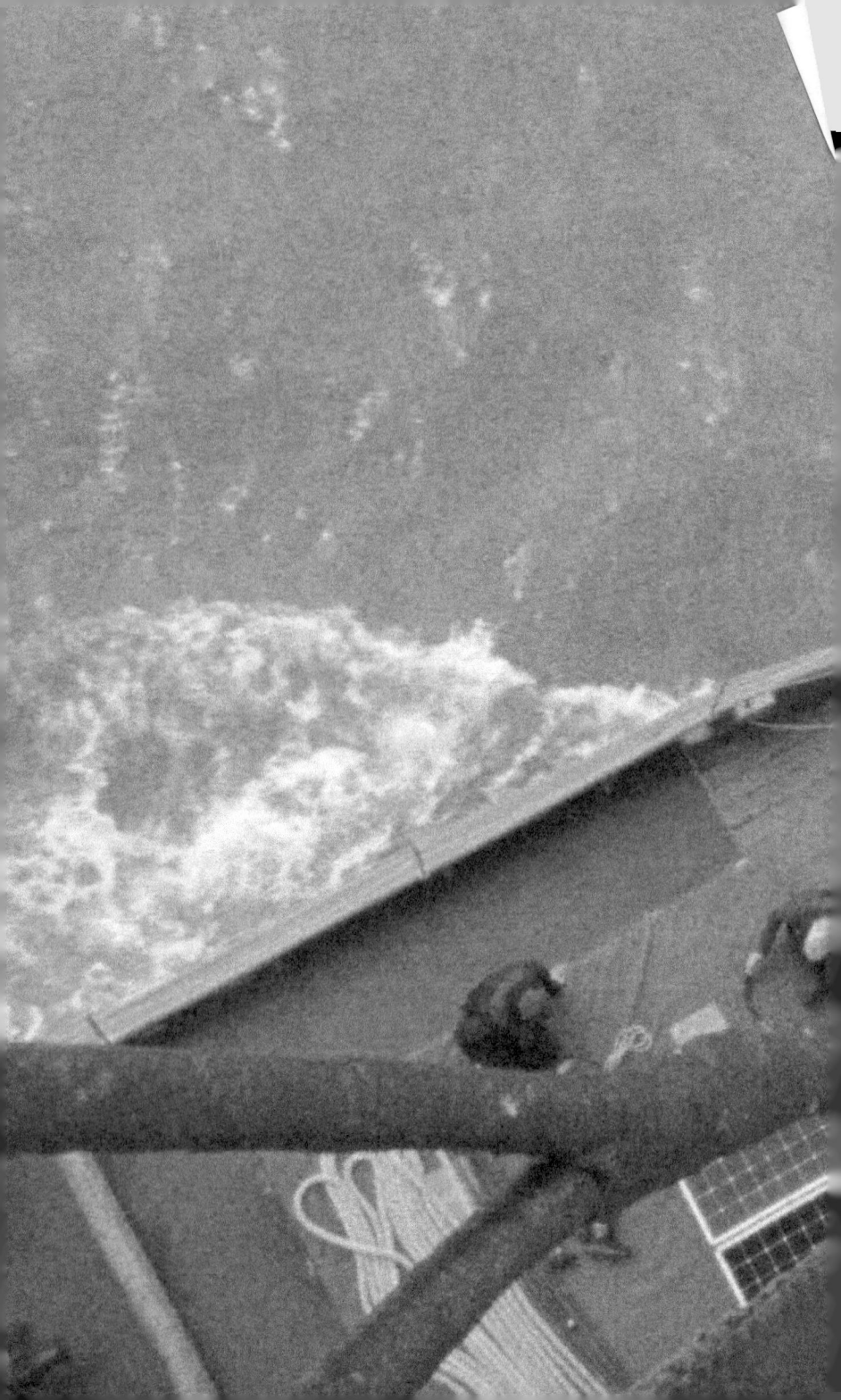

Wind, Tide & Oar: Encounters with Engineless Sailing

This edition was first published in the United Kingdom in 2024
by The New Menard Press

ISBN 9789083384122
First edition, April 2024

Text editing by Penny Iremonger, copy editing by Ilse van Oosten
Typeset in Garamond Premier Pro
Illustrations © 2024 Cessa Rauch
Book design by Martijn Dentant, Armée de Verre Bookdesign, Ghent, Belgium
Printed and bound in in Great Britain by CPI Group
Interior and cover photographs © Huw Wahl
Distributed by InPress Ltd Newcastle upon Tyne

This book was published complementary to the analogue film
Wind, Tide & Oar directed by Huw Wahl. For more information see:
www.windtideandoar.com

www.thenewmenardpress.com